Escape from Villingen, 1918

NUMBER FIVE
C. A. Brannen Series

Escape from
Villingen, 1918

Dwight R. Messimer

TEXAS A&M UNIVERSITY PRESS : COLLEGE STATION

The paper used in this book meets the minimum requirements
of the American National Standard for Permanence
of Paper for Printed Library Materials, z39.48-1984.
Binding materials have been chosen for durability.

Library of Congress Cataloging-in-Publication Data

Messimer, Dwight R., 1937–

    Escape from Villingen, 1918 / Dwight R. Messimer.

       p. cm.—(C.A. Brannen series ; no. 5)

    Includes bibliographical references and index.

    ISBN 0-89096-956-6 (cloth)

    1. World War, 1914–1918—Prisoners and prisons, German.
2. Escapes—History—20th century. 3. Villingen-Schwenningen
(Germany)—History, Military. I. Title. II. Series.

    D805.G3 M465   2000

    940.54'7243462—dc21   00-025119

To my grandson,
Aaron Messimer

Contents

Part III: The Escape

Illustrations

Introduction

This is an account of the only mass escape made by American prisoners of war (POWs) during World War I. The makeup of the escape group reflected the makeup of the American Expeditionary Force (AEF) with one exception: the majority of the escapees were aviators. Among the three who got away was Edouard Isaacs, a naval officer who had been brought to Germany as a prisoner aboard the *U-90*. Stubbornly single-minded about escaping, Isaacs was the heart of the Villingen escape. Isaacs's partner was Harold Willis, an American who flew with the Lafayette Escadrille and the only member of that organization to be captured. He too had a strong motive to escape. The third was 1st Lt. George W. Puryear, a Tennessee lawyer turned pilot who pulled a dumb stunt and ended up as a POW. A born risktaker, Puryear broke all the rules on his way to freedom.

Of those who tried to escape but failed, the largest number came from the undeservedly discredited 96th Aero Squadron, the only American aviation unit the Germans captured intact—including its aircraft. The sole representative of the AEF ground forces was 1st Lt. George H. Crowns, an artillery forward observer captured during the 1918 German Marne offensive. Viewed against the statistics of World War I, what these men did was truly exceptional.

The Germans captured 4,480 members of the AEF. Of that number, only forty-four attempted to escape—some of them several times—and only six succeeded in making their way back to Allied lines. Even fewer British POWs attempted to escape. Among those who did was an American, Lt. Pat O'Brien, a Royal Air Force (RAF) pilot who finally crossed into Holland on November 19, 1917, after making three unsuccessful tries. Included in the ranks of the handful of French POWs who tried to escape were three Americans, all enlisted pilots.[1]

Regardless of their nationality or the army in which they served, the overwhelming majority of men who tried to escape were officers. In the case of the AEF, the only enlisted man to escape was Pvt. Frank Sovicki, who crossed into Switzerland on October 8, 1918.[2] The main reason most of the escapees were officers was the conditions under which the Germans confined them. German society was rigidly structured, and that social structure was reflected, and even amplified, in the German Army. In turn, the Germans applied their concept of class structure and privilege to the way they handled POWs. Enlisted POWs were forced to work on roads, in the fields, and in the mines. Officers, on the other hand, were not required to work at all. Officer camps were much less crowded than the enlisted camps. The Germans also offered officers such amenities as canteens, where they could purchase a variety of luxury items including beer and wine. The armies fighting in France authorized officers to have enlisted men for orderlies, and the Germans followed that practice in the camps. With the exception of the punishment and retaliation camps, all officer POW camps in Germany featured a theater and ample recreation facilities, and there were opportunities for the prisoners to take walks outside the camp. Enlisted prisoners had none of those privileges. The result was that officers had much more time to plan and organize escape attempts than did the enlisted POWs, whose workdays often lasted ten or twelve hours.

The fact that most American escapees were aviators was true of both members of the AEF and of Americans serving in the British and French forces. But aviators figure less prominently in accounts of British and French escapes, where the arms are more evenly represented among the escapees.

There were several reasons U.S. airmen made more escape attempts than did officers of the other arms. The most apparent is the aggressive, risk-taking character that marked most airmen, especially pilots. Airmen also were generally more familiar with European geography—especially that part of Europe that was close to the front. Knowing where they were in relation to where they wanted to go gave them greater confidence in their perceived chances for success.

Whatever the reasons, the fact is that nearly 30 percent of the 152 U.S.

Army Air Service pilots and observers captured during World War I made at least one escape attempt. As a group, American airmen caused their guards more problems per capita than any other identifiable group of prisoners. The Germans guarded American fliers more carefully and watched them more closely during transfers from camp to camp than they did non-fliers, and the security at camps where fliers were held was generally tighter.

What is presented here is an account of thirteen Americans who broke out of the POW camp at Villingen in the fall of 1918. With one exception—Willis, a sergeant pilot in the Lafayette Escadrille—all the men were officers, and eleven were aviators. During the five and one-half months between 15 March and 6 October 1918, they collectively made thirty escape attempts. Seven of them actually made it through the wire before getting caught. As a group, they were the most troublesome prisoners in the entire German POW camp system.

Escape from Villingen, 1918

PART I
The Players

Sgt. Harold Willis,
Lafayette Escadrille

Harold Willis was twenty-eight years old, a Harvard graduate, and an architect with the Boston architectural firm Allen and Collins when the Great War started in Europe during the first week of August, 1914. A committed Francophile, he took leave from his employer and joined the American Ambulance Service in France, where he earned the Croix de Guerre and Star for rescuing wounded French soldiers under fire. In 1916 he joined the French Foreign Legion and transferred to aviation, becoming the twenty-fifth member of the Lafayette Escadrille on 1 March 1917. Five and a half months later, on 18 August 1917, he became the only member of the Lafayette Escadrille to be captured.[1]

Willis was shot down near Dun-sur-Meuse while flying a fighter escort mission for a bomber squadron attacking German positions near Verdun. Albatross D.IIIs and D.Vs jumped the French formation, breaking it up. As the formation scattered, the fighters became engaged in a series of individual dogfights and Willis suddenly found an Albatross directly in front of him. "I shot up this fellow," Willis recalled, but then discovered another Albatross on his tail.

Willis pulled back hard on the stick of his Nieuport and executed a half loop followed by a half roll, reversing his direction. But the maneuver, known as an Immelmann, failed to shake off the German and Willis became separated from the rest of his flight. The Albatross's pilot, apparently much more experienced than Willis, continued to stay with the nimble Nieuport as both fighters maneuvered violently in an effort to gain an advantage. Willis soon found himself in real trouble when the German fired a burst that chewed up his engine. But the fight was not over. Willis headed for the deck in a last desperate attempt to escape what had become a pack of Albatrosses on his tail. The sky around Willis's plane seemed filled with machine-gun bullets as the Germans hammered away at the crippled aircraft. Several rounds shattered the Nieuport's windshield and shredded the instrument panel. One round narrowly missed Willis's head, knocking off his goggles.

Luck stayed with Willis as he neared the ground and spotted an open area atop a small hill. Powerless, nose up, and under attack, Willis slammed the Nieuport onto the ground, shedding the undercarriage. As the Nieuport slid across the uneven ground, the propeller snapped off and the lower wings were torn away before the fighter finally came to a halt. Willis was unhurt.

Moments later the German who had shot him down landed near the crash site. Several infantrymen were running toward the Nieuport, but the pilot reached Willis first, which was probably a good thing. Willis described the man as "completely correct and considerate." Both pilots spoke French, and the two had a pleasant conversation while they waited. A short time later a car carrying two more aviators arrived and the Germans took Willis to their squadron's field to have breakfast.

When they arrived, Willis shed his flying suit and revealed that he was not wearing a uniform. Instead he was dressed in a pair of green-striped pajamas and two old sweaters. Willis had seen no need to wear a uniform under his flight suit, and the pajama-and-sweaters combination was much warmer. Now, his unconventional attire proved to be an asset, which the quick-thinking Willis used to his advantage by telling the Germans he was *Lieutenant* Willis. Since he was not wearing a uniform and had no identification card with him, the Germans took his word for it. His claim was validated that evening when Edwin Parsons, a friend and squadron mate, dropped a bundle containing an officer's uniform, money, and a note for Willis behind the German lines. The ruse worked, but he was not happy with his situation.[2]

Believing Willis was an officer, the Germans first sent him to Gütersloh, which was relatively close to the Dutch border. While he was there he con-

Figure 1. Harold Willis, the only member of the Lafayette Escadrille captured by the Germans. This photograph was taken at Villingen on 30 June 1918. Courtesy Isaacs Family Papers

sidered escaping, but his stay was not long enough to put his vague ideas into effect. He then passed through several temporary camps until finally, in December, he arrived at the Eutin military prison.

Eutin was not a regular POW camp. In fact, the Germans did not include the prison in the official list of camps provided to the International Red Cross. Nor did they place it on the list of camps open to inspection by neutral powers. Eutin, located north of Lübeck on a lake called Grosser Plön See, was a maximum-security prison for German soldiers. The Germans sent Willis and a hundred or so other French officers to Eutin in reprisal for something the French had reportedly done to German officer prisoners. Both the Allies and the Central Powers operated reprisal camps as a matter of policy, and Eutin fell into that category during the time Willis was there.

Conditions in Eutin were awful in comparison to the regular officer camps. The Germans confined twenty or thirty officers in a room without lights and with no way to cook their own meals. Shortly after the French POWs arrived, their captors stopped distributing Red Cross parcels to them. From time to time the Germans eased the restrictions and even provided some improvements. But what they gave, the Germans could, and did, take away. Throughout Willis's stay, conditions in the reprisal camp grew worse.

By Christmas, several prisoners were talking about escape and had begun making definite plans. Willis's architectural training proved particularly useful. His drafting and art skills made it possible for him to draw precise copies of maps that had been smuggled into the prison. Moreover, those same skills, combined with his ability to craft models and figures from almost any material, allowed him to construct imaginative hiding places for the maps and other escape equipment he made.

The prisoners continued making plans and preparations through December and into January, 1918, when conditions in the prison became even more severe. After the war Willis told an American Red Cross representative: "At the beginning of the new year things became worse. The full reprisal program was enforced. All water was cut off at nine a.m., and we were permitted to have a fire for only two hours daily. The number of officers in the room was doubled and beds were superimposed in three tiers. Study classes, music, and athletics were forbidden. The electric lights which they had given us in the first weeks of January were extinguished at eight p.m. and we were forced to go to bed at that hour. We were not permitted to walk in the corridors."[3]

Willis and a French officer reconnoitered the prison and discovered a place in the prison's wiring system where the power to both the courtyard and perimeter lights could be cut. Then, one of the prisoners purloined a key that fit the locks to two of the inner doors and the door leading outside from the courtyard from a careless guard. A prisoner who was skilled at working with metal took the key and made a wax impression of it. He then cut a duplicate from a hinge and hammered and filed it until it exactly fit the wax casting.

Eutin was a u-shaped, three-story building with an interior courtyard. Across the top of the u was a thick, fourteen-foot-high wall that completed the courtyard enclosure. A single door through that wall led to the grounds outside the prison, where guards were stationed at regular intervals. The entire perimeter was enclosed by a twelve-foot-high illuminated barbed wire fence that was canted inward at the top. Beyond the fence were more guards and open fields.

The plan called for a support team made up of men who were not escaping to kill the power to the lights both inside the prison and along the perimeter. As soon as the lights were out, the nine prisoners attempting to escape would unlock the two interior doors, race across the courtyard, open the outer door, and sprint for the fence. Three of the escapees, equipped with wire cutters, would then cut through the outer wire and all nine would scoot through the hole they made and scatter into the darkness. Timing was critical and good luck essential if the plan was to succeed.

Through February, 1917, and into March, 1918, the men collected food, drew maps, and manufactured compasses. A few days before the escape, the prisoners organized a twelve-man distraction unit whose job was to create a disturbance when the lights went out. The disturbance was intended to distract the guards in the courtyard and draw them out of position. The escape was set for 2100 hours on 15 March.

At exactly nine o'clock on the night of the fifteenth the support teams killed the power and started their disturbance. Willis then unlocked the door to the escapees' room and the nine men crept into the darkened hallway. But there was a problem. The lights in the courtyard remained on and the men in the darkened hallway could clearly see two guards through the window. Willis unlocked but did not open the door into the courtyard, and the nine men crouched below the window, waiting and ready to go.

At ten minutes after nine the courtyard lights finally went out. Willis flung open the door when the members of another distraction team began shouting and banging on pans and the nine escapees rushed across the darkened courtyard to the outer door. The noise was incredible. German guards were shouting warnings and whistles were blowing the alarm as the guards ran to their posts. The plan, already off schedule, was falling apart as Willis unlocked the outer door and opened it slowly. To his utter consternation, the perimeter was still lighted.

Before Willis could close the door, the man behind him pushed forward and went partially through the opening. Willis grabbed him and roughly jerked him back inside, closing the door at the same time. A moment later the perimeter lights went out, Willis threw open the door, and all nine men raced toward the wire. The members of the wire-cutting team hurriedly snipped the strands, dropped their cutters, and bolted through the opening. Several guards opened fire on the escapees who had made it through the wire as a dozen more guards surrounded the opening, their rifles pointed at the prisoners remaining inside. The volume of fire directed toward the fields outside the barbed wire increased, and Willis, taking advantage of the confusion, scooped up a pair of wire cutters and retreated to the open courtyard door. When no one challenged him, Willis stepped through the door, pulled it closed behind him, and ran across the courtyard to the next door. Without pausing to close it, he lunged across the corridor, crashed through the door into his room, and dove into bed. He was sitting up on his bunk looking bewildered when the lights came on and the room filled with German soldiers.

The three men who made it through the wire were not seen or heard from again. The Germans put the five officers captured at the wire into solitary confinement and were still holding them there when they transferred Willis and several others to Bad Stuer six days later. During the time between the escape attempt and his transfer, Willis made a plaster bust of Ludwig von Beethoven that the Germans allowed him to take to the new camp. Inside the bust were the wire cutters he had picked up, a map of Germany, and a compass.

The camp at Bad Stuer was about sixty-five miles northwest of Berlin and, as prison camps go, very pleasant. Willis told an interviewer after the war that conditions there "were much less rigorous than at other German prison camps. In fact, they were exceptional. We were allowed to walk where we wished in the morning and evening, as well as take a plunge in the lake in front of the camp before breakfast and in the middle of the afternoon. In June we were permitted to buy fishing licenses and to fish in the evening in the lake. I soon got myself very fit, and the freedom of life made it possible for me to collect all I needed for escape."[4]

Willis remained at Bad Stuer until 25 June, when the Germans transferred him to Villingen, the camp where American officers were held. Willis was an American but he was not an officer—and even had he been one, it would have been in the French army. But Willis did not quibble over those small differences. He simply gathered together his few possessions, including the bust of Beethoven, and made the move.[5]

Lt. Edouard Isaacs, USN

The *U-90* was running slowly on the surface, driven forward at five knots by its starboard MAN diesel while the port diesel charged the batteries. The sea was low swell and light chop. The weather was clear and visibility excellent except for a light haze. Kapitänleutnant Walter Remy stood in the conning tower with two lookouts, scanning the moonlit sea. Even though the U-boat was outside the designated Allied danger zone, which meant that there was little chance of a destroyer being in the area, Remy was cautious. There had been too many narrow escapes lately.[1]

At 0024 on 31 May 1918 the starboard lookout reported a ship on the horizon, and Remy immediately trained his glasses in the direction the sailor was pointing. The ship was still partially below the horizon and obscured by the light haze. Estimating the ship's course and speed, Remy ordered both diesels brought on line, increased the speed to fourteen knots, and laid a course to intercept the target. At 0100 he ordered his crew to battle stations and prepared for a surface torpedo attack.[2]

A little over an hour and a half later, Remy identified his target as the former Hamburg-Amerika liner *President Lincoln.* At the same time he saw that the ship was in a convoy with three smaller vessels; there were no escorts. Remy broke off the surface attack at 0248, changed course, and brought the *U-90* to its maximum speed of sixteen knots. He had decided to get ahead of the convoy in order to make a submerged torpedo attack.

Breakfast was being served aboard the *President Lincoln* as the watch changed at 0800. The small convoy, traveling in line abreast made a twenty-degree turn to starboard and settled on the new heading. Two miles away, Kapitänleutnant Remy cleared the U-90's bridge and ordered the crew to dive. Tracking the convoy's movements through the periscope, he ordered the outer doors on torpedo tubes two, three, and four opened when the convoy made a twenty-degree turn to port twenty minutes later. At 0835 Remy selected the *President Lincoln*'s second mast as his aiming point and fired torpedoes from tubes one and two. Sixteen seconds later he fired a third torpedo from tube four. The range was less than seven hundred meters, and all three torpedoes were running true.[3]

Aboard the *President Lincoln*, Lt.(jg) Charles E. Briggs was off watch and leaning on the rail staring at the sea when he saw twin torpedo wakes headed directly for his ship. "Torpedo!" he shouted. The Officer of the Deck, Lt.(jg) Wesley C. Martin, yelled "Hard right rudder!" and threw the alarm switch. Bells clanged throughout the ship and the collision alarm whooped as the bow turned away from the torpedoes. It was too late. The first two torpedoes struck the ship almost simultaneously, followed a few moments later by the third torpedo. The result was catastrophic: The *President Lincoln* went down in less than twenty minutes, leaving the sea's surface littered with wreckage, bobbing heads, rafts, and open boats. Fortunately, the *President Lincoln* was carrying just thirty-one passengers. Nevertheless, the crew brought the total number of people aboard to 696, of whom 685 had managed to abandon ship and were now clustered in the water in three large groups.[4]

Thirty minutes after the *President Lincoln* went down, Remy brought the U-90 to the surface and moved slowly among the swimmers, rafts, and boats, searching for the ship's captain or the senior surviving officer. It was the German navy's policy to locate the senior officers on board ships sunk by U-boats and take them aboard as prisoners of war. Knowing this, most of the ship's officers had shed their coats and hats when they went in the water, and those who had kept them on began discarding them to avoid being recognized as officers. Commander Percy W. Foote, the ship's captain, had disguised himself as a coxswain and was holding the tiller in one of the lifeboats. Many other officers were similarly disguised.[5]

Lieutenant Edouard Isaacs was still wearing his coat and hat when the U-90 came alongside the boat carrying him. Since he was obviously an officer, Remy ordered him aboard the U-boat. Isaacs scrambled onto the submarine's deck and stood looking up at Remy in the conning tower. The two officers saluted and Remy asked Isaacs to point out the captain. Isaacs replied that he thought Captain Foote had gone down with the ship. Remy apparently accepted the answer—after all, the *President Lincoln* had gone down like a rock—and motioned for Isaacs to join him in the conning tower.[6]

The U-boat captain offered Isaacs a glass of sherry, which the American accepted, and they talked for a while about the sinking. However, Remy still was not satisfied that Foote was missing. For the next two hours the *U-90* cruised slowly amidst the wreckage while Remy called down to the men in the water and aboard the rafts and lifeboats, asking if anyone knew the whereabouts of their captain. The answer the Americans gave was always the same: Foote had gone down with his ship. Finally satisfied that Isaacs was telling the truth, Remy told him that he was going back to Germany as a prisoner. He ordered Isaacs below and took the *U-90* out of the area.[7]

Isaacs was a prisoner aboard the *U-90* for eleven days before it docked in Wilhelmshaven on 11 June 1918. During that time he had free run of the submarine. He discussed professional subjects freely with the German officers and was allowed to study the *U-90*'s navigation chart. Remy even allowed Isaacs to keep his navy-issued sidearm, an M-1911 .45-caliber semi-automatic pistol, and its ammunition. Isaacs retained his loaded weapon until 13 June, when a guard at the German naval headquarters took it from him.[8]

As a result of his experience aboard the U-90, Isaacs believed he had acquired information that was vital to the Allies. From the moment he stepped ashore in Wilhelmshaven he was determined to escape and deliver his information to the U.S. Navy's headquarters in London. During the course of the next four months he made nine escape attempts, including a leap from a fast-moving train that nearly cost him his life.

Isaacs's determination reflected his personality and upbringing. The son of French immigrants, he was raised in a family that practiced rigid discipline, worked hard, and devoutly believed in the teachings of the Catholic Church. Isaacs grew up with a strong sense of duty, a powerful moral code, and an iron personal discipline. But he also was opinionated to a fault, believing that his way was the right way, and he tolerated no dissent. It was that feature of his character that landed him aboard the *President Lincoln* instead of aboard a warship.

Isaacs graduated from the U.S. Naval Academy with the class of 1915 and was assigned to the USS *Florida* as the junior gunnery officer. However, what should have been the first step up the ladder of a successful career ended with his transfer to a humdrum assignment aboard a troopship. The fault lay with Isaacs, whose exaggerated opinion of himself put him on a collision course with the *Florida*'s gunnery division chief. When the dust settled, Isaacs found himself aboard the *President Lincoln* as junior gunnery officer.[9]

When Kapitänleutnant Remy took Isaacs prisoner, the twenty-eight-year-old American was five-foot-eight, weighed 150 pounds, and was in excellent physical condition. Twenty weeks later he was thirty pounds lighter and his health had been ruined for life. He was also in line to receive the Medal of Honor.

1st Lt. Blanchard Battle,
Air Service, AEF

Blanchard Battle was twenty-three years old and a Georgia Institute of Technology graduate when the United States declared war on Germany on 6 April 1917. He immediately enlisted in the newly created Officers Reserve Corps and applied for pilot training where he proved to be an exceptional pilot. He completed his preliminary flight training in just five weeks, passed his RMA (Reserve Military Aviator) tests in two days, and was commissioned on 15 October 1917. On 20 November the army shipped him overseas for training as a pursuit (fighter) pilot at Issoudun, France.[1]

But Battle never made it into the cockpit of a pursuit aircraft. Instead, Maj. John N. Reynolds, commanding officer of the newly organized 91st Aero Squadron (Observation), selected Battle and sixteen other pursuit-qualified pilots to fly the much less glamorous Salmson SAL2A2 two-seater observation plane. First Lieutenant George C. Kenney, who went on to command Allied air forces in the Southwest Pacific during World War II, wrote in the official history of the 91st Aero Squadron: "Seventeen pilots, newly arrived from Issoudon, were assigned to the 91st completing the quota of pilots. A more disgruntled crowd of officers can hardly be imagined as these all had been taken from *chasse* training at Issoudon, the hoped goal of every flier, and sent to join an observation squadron."[2]

As if being stuck in an observation plane was not bad enough, on 12 June 1918 Battle was given the particularly unpleasant job of flying the escort aircraft on a photographic mission. Nobody liked flying escort missions. Pursuit pilots hated them because they were dangerous and inhibited their natural, free-roaming tendencies. But at least they flew a plane designed for the job. Battle and his observer, Capt. Joseph F. Williamson, had to do it in an aircraft identical to the Salmson SAL2A2 they were escorting.

The mission called for photographing the area south of Metz, which lay about twelve miles behind the lines. Along their route were two active German fighter fields: Mars-la-Tour, which was south and a little west of Metz, and Bendsdorf, which was east and a little south of the city. Three squadrons equipped with Fokker D.VIIs operated from those fields.[3]

Despite the risks involved, the situation was not all that bad. Captain Williamson was an experienced observer and had considerably more time over the front than did Battle. He had been trained by the French and had been flying as an observer since December, 1917, which is why he was a captain and Battle was only a first lieutenant. Moreover, the Salmson, although not a pursuit aircraft, was no slouch of an airplane. The pilot had a single machine gun mounted on the left side of the fuselage that fired through the propeller arc, and the observer was armed with twin machine guns. The biggest handicap was the Salmson's lack of maneuverability, which made it unsuitable for a swirling dogfight with the agile Fokker D.VIIs. Still, the Salmson had good firepower. If Battle handled the plane skillfully and Williamson did not run out of ammunition, they had a fair chance of surviving.

The two Salmsons took off just after noon from the 91st Aero Squadron's field at Gondreville and passed over the frontline trenches about fifteen minutes later. They flew steadily north at twelve thousand feet, keeping the Moselle River on their right wing, without encountering any German aircraft or ground fire. They arrived over the target area just after 1240 and the camera plane started its run. Battle and Williamson remained two thousand feet above watching for fighters while the other aircraft followed its prescribed route. They saw none. At 1300 the camera plane's observer signaled that he was finished and the two aircraft joined up for the trip home. For some reason, though, they did not go directly back to Gondreville. Instead, they turned west and flew toward Conflans, which was about sixteen miles away and thirteen miles behind the lines. Apparently taking such a side trip was not unusual since neither the pilot nor the ob-

Figure 2. Blanchard Battle (left) *was a 91st Aero Squadron pilot who became a POW after he shot off his own propeller. Edouard Isaacs* (right, seated) *believed he had valuable military information needed by Admiral Sims and the British Admiralty in London. He earned the Medal of Honor for his actions. This photograph was taken at the Karlsruhe main camp on 4 July 1918. Courtesy Isaacs Family Papers*

server of the camera plane commented on it in their postflight reports. They simply extended their reconnaissance flight to include Conflans and everything along the way.

Flak and fighters vigorously defended the city, a major rail center and the target of frequent Allied bombing attacks. This made going there a risky business—especially for two observation planes. Given the risk involved, there must have been a good reason for the two Salmsons being there, although the crew of the camera plane never explained what it was.

They were in level flight at fifteen thousand feet when Battle suddenly nosed his plane over and opened fire with the fixed machine gun. There was no target visible, so he must have been test firing it. Whatever his reason, the result was not what he had expected. He later told an interrogator, "There was evidently some fault in the synchronization for at the first burst the propeller was shattered."[4]

There was a saying among pilots of propeller-driven aircraft that "you don't know how hot the day is until the fan stops turning."[5] For Battle and Williamson, the day got very hot, indeed. They were thirteen miles inside German-held territory with no propeller. Their only hope was to glide back. After signaling to the crew of the photo plane that he was in trouble, Battle killed the engine and turned due south. The other pilot waved back and headed off in the same direction, leaving Battle and Williamson alone in the silent sky. The Salmson was a great observation plane, but it was a lousy glider. Battle's goal was the village of Flirey, which lay directly ahead of them and was just three-quarters of a mile behind the Allied lines. The heartbreak for Battle and Williamson was that they came so close to making it.

As they neared the front lines, the Salmson began losing altitude at an alarming rate. They were just behind the German trenches and taking increasingly heavy ground fire when Battle realized they were not going to make it to Flirey. His best hope was to put the plane down in no-man's-land. But they did not have sufficient altitude even for that, and he was forced to land between the enemy's first and second trench lines.

The slow-moving Salmson was an easy target for the German infantrymen and by the time Battle set the aircraft down it was starting to look like a sieve. To make matters worse, the undercarriage tore off when it hit the shell-shattered ground and the Salmson skidded and slued across the torn ground, shedding part of its lower wings along the way. It was a miracle it did not flip over.

Both airmen quickly climbed out of the wreck, and while Williamson dove for cover, Battle tried to set what was left of the plane on fire. The Germans shifted their fire to Battle, who dropped the match he held and threw up his hands in surrender. When the rifle and machine-gun fire from the trenches continued, he dove into a shell hole with Williamson. Both officers were pressed against the side of the crater when a squad of German infantrymen arrived to take them prisoner.

The Germans transported them by car to the field headquarters at Thiaucourt, about ten miles east of where they had come down. They were separated there and Battle was taken to an intelligence officer for the first in a series of daily interrogations. By this point in the war, the German army had established a routine procedure for interrogating freshly captured airmen. The intelligence officer was formal, businesslike, and insistent that his questions be answered. The initial questioning was almost always limited to questions about the squadron, the location of the field from which the pilot came, Allied air strength in the area, and the types of aircraft being used. If the reports made by POWs after the war are to be believed, they never answered such questions. That clearly was not the case, however.[6]

Nearly every pilot carried his identity card in a three-by-four-and-a-half-inch, dark-green leather folder. The Air Service's gold-winged propeller logo was embossed on the front with the words "Rating certificate" above and "Air Service U.S. Army" below it. Inside the folder were two cards that described the bearer. They included the date of his commission, his rank, the unit to which he was assigned, and his photograph. The Germans invariably confiscated these ID folders. In addition, many officers printed their rank, name, and unit on the inside of their Sam Browne belts. Many also carried letters, postcards, and photographs from home when they flew. Those, too, were confiscated. The intelligence officer already knew the type of aircraft the man had been flying, so it was logical for him to assume that the type was common to the prisoner's squadron.

The questions about Allied air strength and the names and locations of airfields were rarely answered. However, there were exceptions. All of the information gleaned from these initial interviews was sent up the line, where other intelligence officers would use it when subjecting prisoners to more sophisticated interrogation methods.

In addition to direct questioning, the initial interrogation officers also threatened prisoners with execution in an effort to obtain information. The ploy involved telling pilots that explosive ammunition had been found in their ammunition belts. They were then warned that since the use of explosive ammunition violated international law, they would be shot if they refused to answer the interrogator's questions.

In Battle's case the interrogation officer varied the story a bit by saying that a note would be dropped behind the Allied lines informing them that "an American pilot, Lieutenant Battle, has been killed in combat." Like every other American pilot, Battle knew there were no explosive rounds aboard his aircraft and that the charge was preposterous. He told his interrogator to "go ahead and drop the note."[7]

To add credence to such threats, interrogation officers often showed the pilots tracer rounds supposedly taken from their ammunition belts. In Battle's case the rounds were brought in by an "armaments officer" who said he had taken them from the Salmson's fixed machine gun. Battle knew that tracers were not explosive rounds and quickly pointed that out to his interrogator. He also noted that the Germans used tracers.[8]

According to the pilots who experienced that line of interrogation, they steadfastly refused to answer any questions. That may be. But the fact is the Germans regularly used the technique, which leads one to believe that they enjoyed at least occasional success with the ploy. After all, they were in control. If they carried out the threat, who would know otherwise? In any event, there is no record of any Allied pilots being shot for having explosive rounds in their ammunition belts.

On 14 June the Germans transferred Battle and Williamson from Thiaucourt to Karlsruhe by train. That was unusual because almost every captured aviator was forced to endure a long series of interrogations before being sent on to a POW camp. For some reason, though, Battle and Williamson skipped the second and third levels of interrogation and went directly to what became known as the "Listening Hotel."

That was certainly of little comfort to Battle and Williamson. On the same day they boarded the train for Karlsruhe, the 91st Aero Squadron's personnel officer recorded that they were the squadron's first losses. In the four months that followed Battle made four escape attempts whereas Williamson made none.

1st Lt. Herbert Allen
"Toots" Wardle, Air Service, AEF

Herbert Allen "Toots" Wardle did not like his first name and preferred to be called by his middle name, Allen, or by his nickname, Toots. A native of Memphis, Tennessee, he enlisted on 30 April 1917. However, getting into the Air Service had not been an easy matter. He was twenty-five years old, a college graduate, and a football player. The problem was his size. He was six feet tall and weighed 180 pounds—twenty-five pounds more than was allowed by the Signal Corps's guidelines.[1]

When the War Department rejected his application, Wardle demonstrated the motivation and tenacity that the army considered an indication of good pilot material: he presented himself to the Memphis Aviation Board without an appointment. A board of officers was quickly convened to hear his appeal. The issue was the relatively limited payload airplanes could carry at that time: every pound made a difference. Captain Arthur P. Christie explained this to Wardle, fully expecting him to understand the logic. But Wardle saw things in a different light. He replied that if the margin between getting a plane off the ground or not getting it off the ground was just twenty-five pounds, then the country was in a hell of a fix. The officers hearing his appeal agreed and approved his request.[2]

Wardle completed pilot training in November, was commissioned a first lieutenant, and went to France for advanced pilot training. However, instead of receiving advanced training, he ended up as a ferry pilot flying new aircraft from England to Orly Field in France, and then from Orly to distribution centers or to frontline units. He never flew over the front lines as he was not combat trained and the planes he flew were either unarmed or carried no ammunition.

On 26 June 1918, Wardle and another ferry pilot, 1st Lt. John "Rabbit" Curry, had gone to Lympne, England, to pick up two new Sopwith Camels and fly them to Orly. Their return route took them from Lympne to Folkstone, where they were to refuel before crossing the English Channel and flying to Saint-Valéry. There they were to pick up the Somme and fly upriver to Amiens. But the British supplied them with maps covering only the Lympne–Amiens leg of the flight. They had no maps for the Amiens–Orly leg.[3] Normally that would not have posed a serious problem since Orly was almost due south of Amiens next to Paris. It was a relatively simple matter to fly that leg using a compass, dead reckoning, and landmarks. All the pilot had to do was find Paris and Orly would be on the other side.

The operations officer at Lympne had been very optimistic when they took off. "Quite simple," he told them as he handed each pilot his aerial map. "Right turn at Amiens and off you go along 184°. Can't miss Paris."[4] It sounded easy but reality was a bit different. The flight across the Channel posed no serious problems unless the weather turned sour or they had engine trouble. Then, once they reached Amiens, it was just another seventy-five miles to Paris. Their only real concern was that by the time they reached Orly their fuel tanks would be nearly empty.

The trip from Lympne to Folkestone took nearly two hours. The weather to that point had been clear, but by the time Wardle and Curry finished refueling thick cloud formations had begun to form over the Channel. Neither pilot liked the looks of the weather ahead, and they discussed the idea of waiting for it to improve. In the end, they decided to go on since there was no way to know when the weather would get any better. There was also the possibility that the clouds did not extend over France.

Despite their concern, the Channel crossing proved uneventful. They made landfall on schedule and found the coast clear except for a few scattered clouds. The Somme was right where they expected it to be, and they changed course to follow the river to Amiens. Then the plan started coming apart. As they approached Amiens the weather became "very misty and cloudy," with steadily decreasing visibility. Wardle told a postwar interrogator that they "had to fly at 2,000 feet to be able to see at all."[5]

Despite the sloppy weather they found Amiens. Then something went wrong. Instead of turning right, Wardle continued flying east toward the German lines. After the war Wardle said that the wind may have pushed his Camel eastward or he may have had a problem with his compass. He even suggested that it might have been a combination of both. Although both explanations are unlikely, something clearly was wrong.

Curry, having made the right turn, suddenly realized his companion was not with him. Aghast, he watched as Wardle's Camel continued eastward. Curry banked left, opened the throttle, and quickly caught up with the errant Camel. He tried to signal Wardle but poor visibility or Wardle's inattention frustrated the attempt. Curry then tried to fly in front of Wardle's Camel in an attempt to "head him off." That too failed and the Camel disappeared into the clouds.[6]

Wardle first noticed he was in trouble when German antiaircraft guns opened up on him. Banking the Camel sharply to head back the way he had come, he flew directly into a flak burst. The explosion knocked his airplane on its nose and drove a shell fragment into the engine. The plane spun wildly downward and Wardle did not manage to regain control until he was about a hundred feet above the ground. German machine gunners then shot his Camel to pieces as he pulled out of the dive. He was lucky it did not burn—and even luckier that he was not hit. He crashed on a railroad track well behind the German lines, suffering a broken nose and a split lip. He was still strapped in the wreckage when a German infantry squad surrounded the aircraft and took him prisoner.

The Germans moved Wardle to the rear fairly quickly and without subjecting him to the usual interrogation routine. They could not accuse him of carrying explosive machine-gun bullets because there was no ammunition in his plane. Furthermore, since he did not belong to a combat unit, the Germans had little interest in him. He passed through a series of temporary camps and prisons in France before being loaded aboard a train bound for Landshut on 30 July. There were seven other Americans with him, including James Norman Hall, who later coauthored *Mutiny on the Bounty*. The train also carried two hundred British prisoners the Germans were distributing to camps throughout southern Germany.

The train was made up of third-class coaches and was used to transport German soldiers to and from the front. The coaches all had doors on both sides at each end, and there were two rows of forward-facing wooden benches separated by an aisle ran the length of each car. German soldiers going on leave filled most of the cars. The middle cars were reserved for the officer prisoners. Four guards were assigned to each of the coaches carrying prisoners—two at each end. A single bench immediately next to the end of the car was reserved for them. The guards were either wounded soldiers who were still not fully fit for duty or members of the Landsturm— a reserve force made up of men who were too old or otherwise unfit for frontline duty. Despite their age and physical condition, the guards were, for the most part, vigilant. They had good reason to be: Losing a prisoner could result in their own imprisonment or assignment to an infantry unit at the front. Still, there were lapses—and it was those lapses for which every prisoner bent on escape watched. As the train traveled through the Black Forest, Wardle saw such a lapse in the attention of the guards' on his coach. When the train left Karlsruhe it passed through Pforzheim and then turned south toward Claw, where the line branched off to the west. As the train moved south it came within eighty miles of the Swiss border.

The cars were full but not overcrowded, and everyone had an assigned seat. But there were always prisoners moving up and down the aisle, either going to and from the lavatory located at one end of the car or visiting with a friend who had been assigned to another seat. The constant shuffling along the aisles had the effect of distracting the guards. The movement was deliberate, intended to mask forbidden activity—of which there was a great deal.

Wardle had already made a friend, Capt. Charles C. Cook of the Royal Air Force (RAF). When the time came to board the train, Cook slipped out of the British group and joined the Americans boarding the train with Wardle. Cook knew the geography of the area they were passing through and suggested to Wardle that this might be their best opportunity for an escape attempt. But neither man was prepared to escape. They had had little to eat, they carried no maps or compass, and they were in uniform. Nevertheless, both were anxious to get away and they made a pact to jump from the train if the chance presented itself. Their plan, formed on the spur of the moment, was to go out through the exit doors at the end of the coach. Wardle would go out one side and Cook would go out the other. After the train was out of sight they would join up and head for Switzerland.[7]

Shortly after the train left Claw and headed east, it slowed to about twenty miles per hour. Wardle and Cook stood up as soon as the train began to slow and worked their way toward the end of the line of men waiting to use the car's only lavatory. As they moved along the aisle, they motioned for others to stand in line so that they were always at the end. Their goal was to create a line extending from one end of the car to the other.[8]

A guard was stationed in front of the door opening onto a platform at the end of the car where the lavatory was located. On his left and right were the doors through which passengers boarded and exited the coach. He was responsible for keeping prisoners from getting out onto the platform between the cars and for preventing anyone from escaping through either of the exit doors. Directly in front of the door guard was the next prisoner waiting to use the lavatory. Another guard stood at the open door to the lavatory keeping an eye on what was happening inside. His job was to prevent prisoners from escaping through the small lavatory window.

A single guard stood in front of the platform door at the other end of the coach, where the lavatory line now ended. Just as at the opposite end, there were exit doors on either side of him. A second guard sat facing forward on the bench to his left front. What had caught Wardle's and Cook's attention was that the end of the lavatory line extended past the seated guard. The last three men in line thus had only one guard watching them.

As they stood at the end of the line behind the seated guard, and the door guard was just inches behind Wardle. At the critical moment Wardle whispered, "now," and threw himself backward. His weight and sudden movement knocked the guard in front of the platform door to the floor. Wardle spun left, grasped the handle of the door on the left, flung it open, and leaped into space. Cook in turn leaped over the guard on the floor, opened the right-hand door, and jumped.[9]

Wardle hit the ground feet first facing in the direction the train was traveling. His forward momentum pitched him forward, arms spread, onto the rocky roadbed. Skinned up and a bit out of breath but otherwise unhurt, he got to his feet and started running in the opposite direction.[10] Cook hit the ground with his left foot first and pitched forward onto his left side, somersaulting as he went. He rolled off the roadbed and down the right-of-way embankment. Slightly dazed, he sat up and looked around. Wardle, who was on the other side of the tracks, was nowhere to be seen. Cook wondered if the American had made the jump. As he got to his feet he considered climbing back up the embankment to hunt for Wardle but settled for shouting his friend's name. Hearing no answer, Cook headed off into the forest.[11]

Meanwhile, Wardle had run back along the tracks for about a hundred yards. Behind him the train had come to a halt and troops were pouring out of the cars. He quickly crossed the tracks and slid down the embankment. He looked to his left in the direction that Cook should have been but saw no sign of him. Figuring that his friend had either not made the leap or had been hurt, Wardle turned and ran along the embankment, away from the train. Noncommissioned officers (NCOs) quickly took command of the search and ordered the soldiers to spread out. Some were sent down both sides of the embankment while others ran down the tracks. Squads fanned out in the forest on both sides of the tracks and began systematically searching the area.

Wardle could hear the troops moving behind him, but he was far enough away that he could not see them. Still, he could tell that the troops coming down the top of the embankment were getting very close. It was only a matter of time before they got ahead of him, came down into the trees, and started searching back along the track. He had two choices: He could strike off through the forest at a right angle to the tracks and hope to get outside the search area, or he could find a place to hide, let the searchers pass by, and then continue south. While trying to decide what to do, Wardle stumbled into a brush-choked culvert. He had found his hiding place. He quickly burrowed into the brush.[12]

The Germans moving along the top of the embankment finally reached a point they figured was beyond the distance the fugitives could have covered. The NCO in charge of the group left six men on the embankment and ordered the rest to form into two groups and search among the trees on both sides of the embankment as they headed back toward the train.

Most of the soldiers involved in the search were frontline veterans headed home on leave. However, a substantial number of Landsturm troops serving as train guards were assisting them. It was Wardle's misfortune that the latter discovered him.

Four soldiers working together found the brush-choked culvert and began to carefully search it. They soon spotted Wardle lying facedown at the bottom and ordered him to come out. As he clambered up to where they stood waiting, one of the men hit him in the small of the back with the butt of his rifle. The blow knocked forward and then they all began beating him. The four Germans pounded his body with their rifle butts, knocking him to the ground. He was lucky he was not killed or badly injured—and even luckier that a veteran frontline NCO showed up and ordered them to stop.[13] Bruised and bleeding, Wardle was marched back to the train at bayonet point.

1st Lt. Carlyle "Dusty" Rhodes, Air Service, AEF

When he joined the army at age twenty-four, Carlyle "Dusty" Rhodes, a wealthy young man from Terra Haute, Indiana, was already a hot pilot. He learned to fly at the Wright Flying School at Hempstead, Long Island, and earned an Aero Club of America aviator's certificate before enlisting in the Officers Reserve Corps in April, 1917. Thanks to his prewar pilot training he was able to complete flight school in record time, earning a first lieutenant's commission and a slot in the first advanced pursuit class at Issoudun in the process. His performance at Issoudun earned him a place among the first eighteen pilots assigned to the newly organized 95th Aero Squadron (Pursuit).

Not only was Rhodes a hot pilot, but his squadron mates rated him as one of the 95th's more colorful characters. When the squadron was sent to the Cazaux gunnery school in March, 1918, Rhodes, not satisfied with the officers' quarters there, rented a small villa near the village of Arcachon. A fellow squadron member, Harold Buckley, recalled that Rhodes found the quiet there that "enabled him to design the uniform that made him famous, a garment which broke every tradition of the American Army, but so cleverly that the regulations couldn't touch him. Later by removing his hat, he was able to pass a few feet away as an officer of any of the Allied Armies according to the exigencies of the moment."[1]

The 95th moved to Toul after completing gunnery training. There the pilots got their first taste of combat and the squadron suffered its first casualties. But Toul was a quiet sector, and the pilots lived comfortably between patrols, the more so thanks to the presence of a nearby hospital staffed by "a swarm of beautiful maidens."[2] The aviators soon discovered gay dogs among us, lady killers who at the end of the day could be seen sneaking off with a sheepish grin under cover of dusk boots mightily polished, hair plastered down and caps at a devilish angle. This naturally led to occasional festivities which were agreeable interludes from the business of war. But it was going too far when some of our amorous lads attended a dance at a maternity hospital, next to a ward of war babies facetiously named by the nurses, Joffre, Pershing, Foch and Petain, in lieu of no names at all. Happily we were not long in this sector so we were spared the sight of Russ Hall, McKeown or Rhodes coming down from a patrol to wheel Joffre, Pershing and Foch in the park for a sunning.[3]

On 28 June the squadron moved into the palatial Château Touquin and three days later began flying regular patrols over the Château-Thierry front. The Germans put up little opposition at first, which was good because it gave the 95th's pilots time to become familiar with the landmarks between Château Touquin and Château-Thierry. However, that all changed on 5 July.

Lieutenants John Mitchell, Waldo Heinrichs, Carlyle Rhodes, and Sydney Thompson flew the evening patrol between Mezy and the Forêt de Villers-Cotterêts. At that time the 95th Aero Squadron was still equipped with French Nieuport 28s. Rhodes, Mitchell, and Heinrichs were all experienced combat pilots, having between them more than three hundred hours over the front. Thompson was a novice who had been in the squadron for a month but had less than two hours over the front. The mission turned out to be his first and last aerial combat action.

Behind Château-Thierry the Americans ran into a pair of Rumpler two-seaters escorted by eight Fokker D.VIIs. The D.VII was a formidable fighter and the Americans were outnumbered two to one. Despite the odds, the Americans attacked the German formation. Almost immediately they found themselves in deep trouble. Mitchell described their situation as being in a "virtual hornet's nest of Fokkers."[4] Thompson was shot down before "he even had a chance," his Nieuport burning fiercely as it fell.[5] Lieutenants Heinrichs and Mitchell teamed up to shoot down one of the D.VIIs before they were in turn attacked by four others. Rhodes shot a Fokker off Heinrichs's tail, then looked back and saw another Fokker on his own.[6]

The German had Rhodes right where he wanted him and proceeded to shoot the Nieuport to pieces. Rhodes headed for the ground, his rudder controls shot away and the engine smoking and spewing oil. The German stayed on him until the Nieuport hit the ground, shed its undercarriage, and slued to a stop in an artillery-torn field. Rhodes scrambled out of the cockpit and ran toward the sun. The field in which he had crashed was pocked with shell holes and Rhodes assumed he was in no-man's-land. Using the setting sun as his guide, he ran toward what he thought were the Allied lines. Ahead of him he saw what was obviously a trench. The fact that the barbed wire entanglements were on the opposite side of the trench should have been a clue that he was behind the German lines. But Rhodes had no experience in the trenches, so that detail failed to register with him as he raced across the field, fully expecting to be shot in the back at any moment. Thinking he had reached safety, he unhesitatingly jumped into the trench.

It is hard to imagine who was more surprised: the Germans sitting in the trench when the American suddenly dropped in on them, or Rhodes when he found himself surrounded by German infantrymen. In any event, the Germans reacted first. Two huge infantrymen leaped on the stunned aviator and wrestled him to the ground. Rhodes did not resist, especially when a third soldier pressed a bayonet against his chest. An officer appeared on the scene while Rhodes was still flat on his back and told him to stand up. Rhodes had the good sense to salute, which eased the tension and pleased the German, who properly returned the salute.

While a soldier searched him for a weapon, the officer motioned for a sergeant who spoke English to question Rhodes. The sergeant asked if he was British and Rhodes replied that he was an American, at the same time opening his flight suit to expose the USR devices on his uniform collar. That piece of information seemed to make a great difference. The officer's attitude became decidedly more friendly, and the sergeant interpreter relayed an invitation for Rhodes to join the officer for dinner at the regimental mess. It turned out to be the last good meal Rhodes would have for several months.

While Rhodes was being escorted to dinner, Heinrichs and Mitchell landed back at their field and made their reports while the rest of the squadron's pilots stood around them, listening. Harold Buckley recalled that the score for the day was "one dead German, Syd Thompson down in flames, Rhodes gone—disquieting was not the word."[7]

Rhodes may have been down, but he was far from out. He started planning to escape almost from the moment the Germans sent him to the rear. He made three attempts, his second being a jump from the train carrying him from Landshut to Villingen on 15 August. He managed to evade the Germans for six days before he was recaptured. Of the thirteen men who later took part in the mass escape at Villingen, Rhodes was second only to Isaacs in his determination to get back to the Allied lines.

1st Lt.
William W. Chalmers,
Air Service, AEF

William Chalmers perfectly fit the profile the U.S. Army had drawn up for selecting its pilot candidates. He was five-foot-seven, weighed 136 pounds, and was in excellent health. In addition, he was a college graduate—Middlebury College class of 1913—with a Bachelor of Science degree in engineering. Moreover, he had played varsity football all four years he was at Middlebury, and the army placed great value on athletic ability. The son of a doctor, Chalmers was teaching high school mathematics in Hartford, Connecticut, when America declared war on Germany on 6 April 1917. He was twenty-seven when he enlisted in the Officers Reserve Corps a little over a month later and was accepted into the pilot training program.[1]

One of the brightest stars in the army's School of Military Aeronautics at Ohio State University, he was sent directly from Ohio State to France for all his flight training. Chalmers fulfilled the army's expectations of him and was slated to be one of the first fourteen pilots assigned to the newly created 95th Aero Squadron, but he fell ill on the day the assignments were made and was replaced by another pilot.[2] The setback was short-lived, however, and one year after he enlisted, Chalmers became a frontline pursuit pilot in the famed 94th Aero Squadron.[3]

On 9 July 1918 two flights from the 94th were assigned to escort a 1st

Aero Squadron photoreconnaissance plane over the front. The 1st Aero Squadron pilot and his observer were undoubtedly feeling secure as their Salmson started its camera run, knowing that a eleven Nieuport 28s from the 94th were a thousand feet above them. First Lieutenant Eddie Rickenbacker led the six-plane flight and 1st Lt. James Meissner led the other five. Chalmers was in Meissner's flight.

The mission had crossed Château-Thierry and turned northwest to approach Épaux, the starting point of the triangular photographic run. After completing the first four-mile leg, Épaux to Priez, the planes turned northeast for the second four-mile leg, Priez to Grisolles, which was ten miles inside the German lines.

At 0950, as the group passed over Grisolles and started on the third leg, they spotted a pair of Rumpler two-seaters a mile and a half away over Rocourt. The reaction was immediate. The Nieuports abandoned the Salmson and turned toward Rocourt to attack the Rumplers. Rickenbacker's flight went after one and Meissner's flight went for the other. There was time for only one pass because they dared not leave the Salmson alone for long that deep in enemy territory. In fact, they should not have left him alone at all. Rickenbacker's led his flight in a diving attack on its target, all six Nieuports in line astern formation. First Lieutenant Alden B. Sherry piloted the last plane in Rickenbacker's flight and the Rumpler was still unscratched when his turn came to fire. Sherry squeezed off a long burst at the German, who by then was doing some very fancy flying, but missed. As he pulled up to rejoin his flight he saw that Meissner's planes were also reforming.

Meissner's flight had also made a diving, line astern attack—but with much more dramatic results. First Lieutenant Robert Z. Cates was in the third plane in line, and when his turn came to fire the Rumpler was down to under three thousand feet and already burning. Cates fired fifty to sixty rounds at the Rumpler and pulled up. Chalmers, in the last plane in the string, watched as the flaming Rumpler spun downward toward the ground, hoping "to see the crash."[4] He wanted to confirm its location and thus improve their chances of having the kill confirmed.

While he was stooging around, Chalmers lost contact with his four companions, who had rejoined the Salmson and were heading back toward the Allied lines. But Chalmers was not alone—the Rumpler also had an escort. The four German fighter pilots were too late to save their charge but they arrived in time to shoot down one of the guilty Nieuports. The man who got credit for downing Chalmers, Vizefeldwebel Otto Rosenfeld, was already an ace. The hapless American turned out to be his thirteenth and last "kill."

Chalmers saw the four Fokker D.VIIs coming at him at about the same altitude and turned to meet them. The lead Fokker fired a burst that hit his engine and banked away. The Nieuport's engine coughed and sputtered but continued to run as Chalmers tried to turn toward his next attacker. Rosenfeld attacked from the right side as the crippled Nieuport staggered through the turn and fired a burst that reduced its engine to scrap. The plane's nose dropped and the Nieuport plunged downward. Rosenfeld, seeing his victim fall, rolled his Fokker over, pulled it into a tight, diving turn, and locked onto its tail, firing all the way down.

Chalmers had built up plenty of airspeed and he struggled to pull out of the dive. Skimming along just above the ground, the Nieuport sheared off its landing gear on a fence, slammed onto the dirt, and plowed across an open field, shedding its lower wings and tail along the way. When the wrecked plane finally ground to a stop, its upper wings were broken and drooping down, the engine had torn loose, and the instrument panel was twisted forty-five degrees. It was pure luck that Chalmers survived the attacks and walked away from the crash.

As he climbed from the shattered wreckage, a squad of German infantry whose mood was decidedly unfriendly surrounded him. Chalmers spoke German fairly well and understood what the soldiers were saying. Apparently the German two-seater had crashed near their position, killing both the pilot and the observer. One would think that the wholesale butchery on the western front would have hardened those German soldiers. In most cases they probably did accept death without so much as a shudder. But for some reason the Rumpler's crash and the immolation of its occupants had incensed them, and they were seriously discussing shooting Chalmers on the spot.

The situation was growing very ugly when Rosenfeld and Leutnant Erich Raabe landed in the field. The arrival of the two Fokkers distracted the soldiers, who watched the aircraft roll to a stop and the pilots climb down. The thing that really helped Chalmers at this point was that Raabe was an officer, and he took charge at once.

Neither of the pilots spoke English, but Chalmers's German was good enough to communicate to them that he was uninjured. While Raabe conversed with Chalmers, Rosenfeld walked to the remains of the Nieuport and cut the "Hat-in-the-Ring" emblem from the side of its fuselage. After the formalities and pleasantries were over, the German pilots took their leave and turned Chalmers over to a cavalry officer who had appeared on the scene. They exchanged salutes all around and the pilots climbed back into their Fokkers. Chalmers was led away for interrogation as the two fighters lifted off.

Less than an hour later Otto Rosenfeld was dead. After leaving the crash site, he and Raabe rejoined their flight near Château-Thierry and moments later attacked a group of 95th Aero Squadron Nieuports. During the melee that followed, 1st Lt. Sumner Sewall attacked Rosenfeld's aircraft. According to Sewall he "fastened himself" on the Fokker's tail but the German was too agile to get a hit. Either Rosenfeld was low on gas or out of ammunition because he suddenly dove away "for home and the Vaterland as fast as he could go." [5]

Sewall stayed with him, still unable to score any hits, until the two fighters were roaring across France barely a hundred feet above the ground. Sewall suddenly became aware of the fact that he was alone and some twenty miles behind the German lines. In a final desperate attempt to bring the Fokker down, he climbed to a point just above and behind Rosenfeld, dropped his nose, and fired a long burst into the enemy aircraft. The result was instant and catastrophic. The Fokker's nose dropped and the plane flew into a village at full power, demolishing a building and strewing fiery wreckage down the street. Sewall pulled up and headed home.

Unaware that his loss had been avenged, Chalmers was already thinking about escape. When the first opportunity presented itself eighteen days later, Chalmers seized it. He remained free for nine days before the Germans caught him. He would do it again.

Maj. Harry Brown
and the 96th Aero Squadron

On 10 July 1918 the 96th Aero Squadron (Bombardment) lost six crews and their aircraft on one mission. It was the largest single-day loss of any American Air Service unit up to that time, and the only instance in which the Germans captured an entire squadron and its aircraft intact. The squadron's status as the first American day bombardment squadron was loaded with political significance and its loss was a serious blow to American prestige. As a result, news of the humiliating loss was quickly suppressed so that no information got to the press.

The man who led the 96th that day was Maj. Harry Milford Brown, a twenty-seven-year-old West Point graduate whose career seemed to be taking off. At least that was how it looked until 10 July.[1] Major Brown, like most of his Air Service contemporaries, was relatively small in stature, and his baby face made him look much younger than he was. But looks were deceiving. Beneath his cherubic exterior was a personality that would neither suffer fools nor tolerate anything less than maximum effort from his subordinates. His men described his temperament as "mercurial."[2]

Anxious to make his mark, Brown ignored obviously bad weather on the morning of 10 July and took off to bomb the rail yards at Conflans. Instead of finding the target, his six-plane formation arrived over Koblenz less than an hour after takeoff, completely lost. After bucking ninety mile per hour head winds, the Breguet bombers began running out of fuel and one by one landed in Germany.

Brown went down first at 2110 near Immerath, on a line between Aachen (then known as Aix-la-Chapelle) and Düsseldorf. When they landed, Brown thought he and his bombardier, 2d Lt. Harold McChesney, might be in France because the country resembled the area around Commercy. They were soon disabused of that notion when they questioned a passing peasant and discovered the man was German. Aware that they were down behind enemy lines, the two airmen set about destroying the bombsight and burning their maps and documents. While they were in the middle of that work, a crowd of villagers approached the plane and McChesney drove them off with machine-gun fire.[3]

After driving off the crowd, McChesney smashed the altimeter, compass, and guns but they did not destroy the aircraft. When they heard the sounds of a large mob coming after them, both men ran into a nearby wood. They hid there until 2300, then crawled through the line of searchers and set off for Luxembourg. Brown and McChesney were on the run for nine days before the Germans captured them near the Luxembourg border.

Lieutenants Joseph Mellen and Rowan Tucker were in the second plane to go down. They landed near Euskirchen, forty miles southwest of Bonn, and were immediately captured. They did not have time to destroy their aircraft.[4]

The next two airplanes to land set down at about the same time just seven miles apart. Lieutenants Robert Browning and James Duke landed at Cochem on the Mosel River among a squad of soldiers who captured the Americans before they had a chance to burn their aircraft.[5] The other plane, manned by Lieutenants Herbert Smith and George Ratterman, landed outside nearby Burg. They too failed to destroy their plane because they were "just beginning to debate their exact whereabouts" when they heard a large group of people coming. Both men ducked into some bushes and waited while the crowd of civilians, a handful of soldiers, and two policemen examined the aircraft. After a short wait the two Americans, deciding that trying to escape without a compass, map, and food was futile, came out of the bushes and surrendered.[6]

Lieutenants Henry Lewis and Caxton Tichener landed at Lutzerath at 2140 and found that the countryside was already alerted. They were

Figure 3. Rowan Tucker, 96th Aero Squadron. Tucker was an observer/ bombardier, which is why he is wearing a half wing. The Germans captured Tucker and his entire squadron with their aircraft intact on 10 July 1918. Courtesy Puryear Family Papers

"quickly surrounded and taken to the local jail before they could destroy their aircraft.[7]

The last to land were Lieutenants Durward MacDonald and Alfred Strong, who set down near Kirchberg, twenty-four miles southwest of Koblenz. Thinking they were in France, MacDonald waited with the plane while Strong walked to a nearby village to ask for directions and use a telephone to notify the squadron of their whereabouts. However, instead of returning with information, he came back at the head of an infantry squad. The Germans captured MacDonald and their still-intact Breguet bomber.[8]

As the daylight on 10 July faded and turned to night, the duty officer recorded the following entry in the squadron log: "Six planes left at 6:05 PM, target . . . Conflans. 11:30 PM no word of planes."[9] The following day the duty officer recorded: "At 4:00 PM 96th headquarters received an extract of an intercepted German radio message: 'Out of a squadron of six American planes which intended to attack Koblenz, we captured five together with their crews. It is believed the sixth plane landed within German lines farther south than the others.'"[10]

The German intelligence officer who sent that message was correct in his assumption that the sixth plane was down inside Germany. He just had the direction wrong. At I Corps headquarters, Col. William "Billy" Mitchell, the corps air officer, wrote in his diary:

> He lost his way in the fog and landed in Germany with every ship intact. Not one single ship was burned or destroyed and the Germans captured the whole outfit complete. This was the most glaring exhibition of worthlessness that we have had on the front. The Germans sent back a humorous message, which was dropped on one of our airdromes. It said, "We thank you for the fine airplanes and equipment which you have sent us; but what shall we do with the major?" I know of no other performance in any air force in the war that was as reprehensible as this. Needless to say we did not reply about the major, as he was better off in Germany at that time than he would have been with us.[11]

Mitchell's judgment of Major Brown, though understandable, was not entirely accurate. Brown and McChesney did not give up easily. They eluded the Germans for nine days before their luck ran out. They would try to escape again at Villingen. Mellen, Strong, Tichener, and Tucker all made multiple escape attempts before they were sent to Villingen, and they would also take part in the mass escape from that camp.

2d Lt. George H. Crowns, 10th Field Artillery

At fourteen minutes after midnight on 15 July 1918 the Germans hurled forty-seven divisions against the front between Château-Thierry and the Argonne Forest. Advancing behind the most ferocious artillery bombardment of the war, the Germans crossed the Marne and drove toward Épernay. Battery A, 2d Battalion, 10th Field Artillery, was located on the 3d Division's right, near the Janvier Farm, with orders to sweep the slopes in front of the American 38th Infantry Regiment. Unbeknownst to the gunners in Battery A, they were directly in the path of the last of a series of massive German offensives in the spring and early summer of 1918 intended to bring an end to the war.[1]

The first sign that Battery A was in trouble appeared twenty minutes after the German barrage opened when the guns lost telephone communication with battalion headquarters and with the battery's forward observation post. Blind, without orders or information from battalion, Battery A's gunners hunkered down under the barrage, which included both high explosive and gas shells. At the first whiff of gas someone started ringing the gas alarm, but the bell was drowned out by the explosions and finally silenced altogether by shell fragments. All along the gun line, men shouted "Gas! Gas!" as they struggled to don their gas masks. German shells continued to rain down around them and the explosions deafened men, overturned guns, and collapsed bunkers. Jagged shell fragments slashed through flesh, mangling and killing men and horses. Calls for corpsmen filled the air, but there were no more corpsmen to answer. The dead lay where they fell and the wounded suffered. Casualties mounted.

Four kilometers forward of the battery's position, 2d Lt. George Crowns and four riflemen in the forward observation post endured the devastating bombardment. For Crowns, the situation held a certain irony. He was a thirty-year-old high school science teacher who had been assigned to the field artillery because the army considered him too old for the infantry. Now, blinded by smoke and dust, his telephone lines to the rear cut, and with German infantry crossing the Marne River in front of his position, Lieutenant Crowns was worried. He quickly scribbled a message describing the situation and asking for orders. Should they stay or should they pull back? Manning the observation post seemed pointless if they could not communicate with the battery. But Crowns had to stay until he was told to leave. He handed the message to one of the riflemen and told him to take it to the battery commander. As the runner disappeared into the darkness, Crowns turned back toward the front and studied the river below him through his binoculars. The Germans had erected a bridge across the river and still more assault infantry was crossing in boats.

In the battery command post, Capt. A. Brigham, Jr., had lost contact with his forward observer, battalion headquarters, and the infantry regiment he was supposed to be supporting. Unable to receive calls for fire, Captain Brigham seized the initiative and ordered his gunners to fire on the battery's predesignated target areas.

At 0200 Sgt. Robert Burroughs, the battalion's mounted courier, arrived at Battery A with a message. Burroughs had ridden three miles through the barrage and both he and his horse were miraculously unscratched. The note he handed Captain Brigham was brief and to the point: "Continue firing at your own discretion."[2]

Brigham hastily scrawled out a reply: "Need more ammunition badly. Send some as soon as you can." He handed the note to Burroughs and saluted. The rider climbed back into the saddle, lay low across his mount's neck, and headed back into the barrage rolling inexorably toward the rear.

By 0230 Captain Brigham's guns were nearly out of ammunition, all his horses were dead, and his unit had lost more than a third of its men. The walking wounded brought forward what little ammunition the battery was getting while the able-bodied manned the guns. The fire from Battery A began to slacken.

At 0300 the headquarters of German Army Group Crown Prince, received the following message from the 10th Division, which was being fired on by Battery A: "All telephonic communications shot to pieces. Enemy artillery in irregular intervals, bombarding heights above division headquarters and ground behind it."[3] The Germans were gaining ground but they were running into unexpected resistance.

At 0345 German aircraft attacked a French light artillery battery located a half-mile behind Battery A. The entire French battery was destroyed, and the French infantry on the 3d Division's right flank was falling back. At 0530 Battery A fired its last round. Captain Brigham wrote in his diary: "Ceased Firing. No results derived from details sent to neighboring batteries and to the rear for ammunition. Brigade ammunition trains (trucks) and battery combat train unable to climb long hill under steady shell fire to reach any reasonable proximity to battery position. French infantry covering our front falling back to disappear in woods behind us."[4]

Four kilometers forward, Lieutenant Crowns and three enlisted men still occupied their useless forward observation post. The situation around them was confused, and it was impossible to tell which of the shapes moving through the darkness were German and which were French. In fact, all the shapes they saw were German. The French had pulled out without telling them.

Shortly after 0530, Lieutenant Crowns observed that Battery A had ceased firing. There were sounds of heavy fighting to his left but it was mostly quiet on the right. Crowns correctly assumed that the Germans had routed the French on the right flank but that the U.S. 38th Infantry was holding on the left. But what about Battery A? Had the guns been pulled back or had they been overrun?

Up to this point the Germans had either overlooked Crowns and his observation post or ignored it. There was no longer any activity to their immediate front and there appeared to be no Germans in the area. Crowns decided the time had come to get out and that the best way to go was to the left, toward the 38th Infantry. He unfolded his map and showed the three riflemen where they were headed. It was as good a plan as anyone could have made under the circumstances. Unfortunately, there was a problem: They had waited too long.

The four Americans had just climbed out of the hole they were occupying when they spotted a platoon of German soldiers advancing up the slope in extended order fifty yards to their front. They looked to the right and left and saw dozens more enemy troops swarming around them. The Germans were too close for Crowns and his men to run, and they were too badly outnumbered to fight. Cut off from their unit, alone and essentially defenseless, the four Americans reluctantly dropped their weapons and slowly raised their hands above their heads.

1st Lt. George W. Puryear, Air Service, AEF

On 26 July 1918 1st Lt. George W. Puryear, a twenty-three-year-old attorney from Gallatin, Tennessee, who had been in the 95th Aero Squadron for just a week, was scheduled to fly an early morning patrol with four other pilots over the front in the Château-Thierry sector. The mission planners expected the patrol to be out for about an hour and twenty minutes at most. However, the weather was a problem. If it closed in, the plan called for the pilots to either turn back or find a safe place to land. But if the weather held, they were to attack any enemy aircraft they came across. German observation planes were particularly important targets.

They passed over Château-Thierry and flew northeast toward Beuvardes, about seven miles away. The ground below was in Allied hands, but a mile east of Beuvardes the front was fluid and not clearly identifiable. As they approached Beuvardes, 1st Lt. Waldo Heinrichs spotted a Rumpler two-seater observation plane headed toward the Allied lines and signaled for the other pilots to prepare to attack.

Despite his best efforts, the Rumpler's pilot could not escape the American Spads. The gunner was mortally wounded during one of the first firing passes, and the pilot realized his chances for survival were almost nonexistent. He nosed over and put the plane into a spin, hoping the desperate maneuver would shake his pursuers and that he could pull out in time and safely land. He was hoping the Americans would then follow the unofficial rule that once a plane was on the ground, the attackers would stop firing at it.

Puryear was firing at the plane as the German pulled out of the spin and headed for an open field. He was still firing when the enemy pilot brought the aircraft's nose up, cut the power, and flared out. The observation plane made a perfect three-point landing and rolled to a stop as Puryear's Spad roared overhead. As Puryear came around for another pass he saw the pilot stumbling across the field with the dead observer across his shoulders. Other than the abandoned Rumpler and the two German fliers, the field appeared to be empty. It was then that he decided to land. Puryear later said of the decision: "I never thought for a moment but what we were in Allied territory, and, in my enthusiasm, landed, as is usual, when a plane is brought down—in your own territory of course."[1]

Puryear gauged the field, decided it looked good, and made a picture-perfect landing. But even as the Spad rolled across the field, Puryear was starting to have second thoughts about what he was doing. "As I taxied around the field I suddenly realized I might be behind the German lines," he later told an army investigator, "so I headed my machine around to face the long way of the field and prepared to take off."[2] He did not make it. The Spad's wheels fell into a shallow ditch and the aircraft pitched forward onto its nose, snapping the propeller. Puryear was overcome by a feeling of uneasiness when he saw the broken propeller and suddenly realized that he might be in enemy territory.[3]

He climbed out of his wrecked Spad and looked around for signs that he was behind friendly lines. There were none. Nor were there any signs of enemy activity in the immediate area—at least none within a hundred yards of where he was standing. He had no watch with him, but the clock on the Spad's instrument panel showed the time to be 0721.

Puryear could hear machine guns firing all around him but none seemed to be firing in his direction. Half a mile away an observation balloon marked with large black crosses rode high above the ground. He took a bearing on it with his pocket compass and thought that he might be in Allied territory. In fact, he was behind the third German trench line.

At about that time a disconcerting new factor entered the picture. German antiaircraft guns were firing at the other three Spads, which were circling overhead. The fact that the guns were firing was not enough to convince him he was inside the German lines, but the fact that they were

Figure 4. George Puryear, 95th Aero Squadron. Puryear was captured after he landed behind the German lines to "accept the surrender" of a German pilot he had shot down. Puryear was the first American officer to escape from the Germans and return to his unit. This photograph was taken at Villingen on 15 September 1918. Courtesy Puryear Family Papers

so close added to his worries. Three thousand feet overhead, his comrades were in a bad spot. The low cloud cover gave the German gunners an accurate estimate of their altitude, and both machine guns and large-caliber antiaircraft guns were firing at them. Heinrichs decided it was time to leave. Puryear watched his companions disappear to the south with growing concern. He was alone, but not for long.

A few minutes later, Puryear watched a lone figure approach his position from a thicket to the south. The man appeared to be unarmed and friendly. At least he did not appear threatening, so Puryear hoped for the best. As the man drew closer Puryear saw that he was bareheaded. His spirits soared: the man might be French! Puryear hailed him in French and the man answered in the same language. He was still standing beside his Spad when the man came up to him. Puryear, still speaking French, asked the stranger where he was. The man told him he was behind the German lines and asked if he was an American officer. When Puryear replied in the affirmative, the man snapped to attention and saluted him. Before Puryear could react to that development he was surrounded by several armed German soldiers who had come up on him from behind.

Puryear became a prisoner of war at 0745 on 26 July 1918, a date that had special significance for him. His father had been a cavalryman with Confederate raider John Hunt Morgan during the Civil War. The senior Puryear was captured in Ohio with Morgan on 26 July 1863, exactly fifty-five years to the day before his son became a POW. The senior Puryear did not remain a prisoner long, however. He escaped. The significance was not lost on the son, and the coincidence became his primary motivation to escape.[4]

PART II

The Camps

Friedrichsfeste, Rastatt

With just two exceptions, Willis and Isaacs, all the men who took part in the mass escape from Villingen passed through Rastatt, which was one of the large distribution camps for Allied officer prisoners in Germany. Wardle was in the prison during the first week in July, all six 96th Aero Squadron crews passed through the camp between 16 and 23 July, Chalmers and Crowns arrived on 24 July, Rhodes was there on 29 July, and Puryear arrived on 3 August.

The camp was actually a fortress prison called Friedrichsfeste. The Germans built the fortress on the bank of the Murg River in 1842 as part of a powerful defensive system to defend against an invasion from France. However, as military technology progressed, Friedrichsfeste's importance declined. By 1900 the Germans had converted the fort into a military warehouse, administrative center, and barracks. In 1915 they turned the fortress into a transit camp, using it as one of three primary reception centers for officer POWs when they reached Germany.[1] The officer POWs remained there from three days to three weeks before being sent to the so called permanent camps located throughout Germany.

The prison was a two story quadrangle with heavily barred and grated windows, solid steel clad doors, and massive locks. The Germans pulled frequent random inspections of the corridors and rooms, and sentries walked regularly spaced beats day and night along the base of the four outer walls. Despite the formidable surroundings, tight security, and rigid discipline, Friedrichsfeste was one of the better camps.

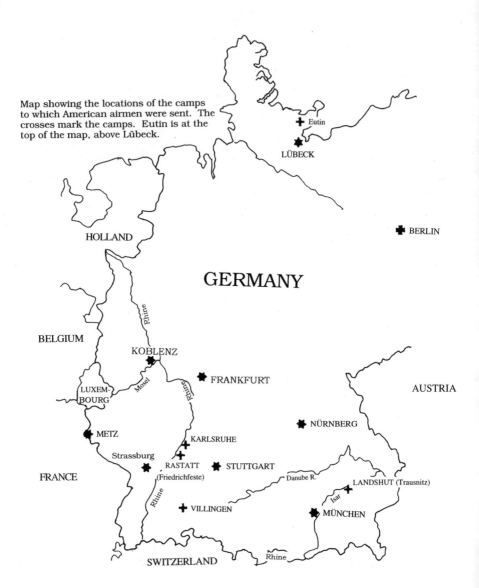

Map showing the locations of the camps to which American airmen were sent. The crosses mark the camps. Eutin is at the top of the map, above Lübeck.

Map 1. Locations of POW camps in Germany, 1917–18. Courtesy Isaacs Family Papers

Each prisoner had an iron bed with flat springs, a real mattress, two blankets, and what passed for sheets. The sheets, which were made of what felt like thin canvas or moderately rough cotton, at least passed for a "sort of sheets."[2] The food at Friedrichsfeste, although not what one would classify as good, was better than the food at the other officers' POW camps. Daily meals included a breakfast of brown bread and acorn coffee, followed by a lunch and dinner of vegetable soup made from carrots, beans, and potatoes. Occasionally the soup included some sort of meat. Although the diet was bland and uninteresting, the quantities doled out in Friedrichsfeste were usually sufficient to ward off serious hunger.

Like all German officers' POW camps, Friedrichsfeste had a canteen where the prisoners could buy a limited variety of items such as milk, tobacco, a few vegetables, and writing paper at exorbitant prices. The Germans also provided for improved hygiene at Friedrichsfeste, where the prisoners had regular access to showers and a large latrine that featured flushing toilets. American doctors who had been captured with British frontline units saw to the prisoners' medical needs.

The prisoners in Friedrichsfeste were housed in rooms located on the top level of the fort's outer walls, twenty five feet above the street below. Guards walked beats along the base of the outside walls, three of which were bounded by narrow streets that separated the old fort from the new part of the city. From the outside, as well as from the inside, Friedrichsfeste, with its high, thick walls, multiple iron reinforced doors, and dry moats, gave the appearance of being escape proof. But in this case, the appearance was deceiving: More prisoners escaped from Friedrichsfeste than from any other German camp.

Sometime in 1915 several enterprising French officers managed to loosen one of the bars in a second-story window and reset it so that the bar could be removed and replaced at will. The French did their work so neatly that the Germans never discovered the loose bar. The guards' inability to discover it is even more surprising when one considers that sixty three men escaped through that window from 1915 to 1918, and its existence was known to literally hundreds of prisoners.[3]

Directly across the street from the window with the loose bar was a cluster of small private holdings called a Siedlung. This collection of shacks and gardens was divided into blocks by a grid of ruler straight footpaths. The Siedlung was a summer and weekend getaway spot for the owners,

Figure 5. Friedrichsfeste in Rastatt as it appeared in 1914–18. The Germans used the former fortress as a POW camp throughout World War I. More escapes were made from this camp than from any other German camp during the war. Courtesy Kurt Kranich

and during the summer months it was almost fully occupied. Beyond the Siedlung was a cluster of houses that formed the last six or seven blocks of built-up area that became the outskirts of the expanding city of Rastatt. Farther beyond those houses lay open country dotted with small farms. The security of the Black Forest was less than three miles away.

The Siedlung created both opportunities and problems for would be escapees. What had formerly been open fields were now covered with buildings and streets that reduced the guards' fields of view from the base of the wall. But those same buildings and streets meant that an escapee had to make his way through a heavily populated area before he reached the Black Forest.

Escapees using the window with the loose bar needed a fairly large support organization, which in practice was relatively easy to organize. Escape through the window typically required a knotted sheet or rope that the prisoner used to lower himself to the street. Several lookouts were needed to warn of the guards' movements, and someone had to pull in the rope and stash it. Timing was critical. The escapee had to time his descent so that he started down just as the sentry disappeared around a sloping buttress at the end of his beat. Once on the rope, the escapee had to reach the ground and conceal himself before the sentry reappeared—which normally occurred in about a minute. Lookouts stationed along the second-floor windows monitored the sentry's movements and sounded a warning if the escapee was in danger of being discovered.

Once on the ground, the escapee flattened himself in the low grass and bushes along the base of the wall while his accomplices hauled the rope back inside. The escapee would remain hidden until the sentry passed back along his beat in the direction of the far corner of the prison, then sprint across the road into the Siedlung. From there he began the long trek toward the Swiss border.

The fact that the prisoners had a relatively easy route out of the prison has to be weighed against the fact that everyone who got out of Friedrichsfeste was brought back. It may have been easy to get out, but it apparently was impossible to stay out.

That was the situation when William Chalmers and George Crowns escaped from Friedrichfeste. Chalmers had spent the two weeks since he had been shot down being shifted from prison to prison until he arrived at Rastatt on 24 July. He hooked up with Lieutenant Crowns, the 10th Field Artillery forward observer who was captured on 15 July, that same day. Crowns, who was plotting an escape attempt three days hence, took an immediate liking to Chalmers and invited him to join him.[4]

At twenty-seven and thirty, respectively, Chalmers and Crowns were older than most of their contemporaries. On the surface they appeared to be fairly well prepared. Their boots were in good shape, which was an important point, and Crowns had acquired a compass and a handdrawn map of the route from Rastatt to Waldshut, on the Swiss border. The map showed little detail but it was geographically correct. They had only a limited amount of food, but they believed it would be enough to get them to Switzerland, a little over ninety miles due south. One problem was that both were still wearing their uniforms, which were hard to conceal and too light for the nighttime temperatures they would encounter. They also lacked any sort of rain gear to keep them dry during the Black Forest's frequent summer showers. Nevertheless, they went out the window on the evening of 27 July.

Chalmers went first and was on the ground in less than thirty seconds. Crowns was just moments behind, starting his descent while Chalmers was still on the rope. They both dropped to the ground without being heard, and the guard never hesitated as he plodded along the wall. Chalmers wasted no time at the base of the wall. As soon as he touched down he cast a quick glance at the guard's back and sprinted across the path.

Crowns joined Chalmers less than a minute later and the two men started walking through the Siedlung. It was nearly midnight and most of the Germans staying there were in bed. But here and there groups of die hard partiers sat in their dark gardens, drinking beer and talking. No one paid any attention to the two men as they passed by in the dark. The closest they came to being detected was when they walked past a man urinating on a tree. The German mumbled a greeting to them and Crowns muttered something unintelligible in reply. The German either did not hear Crowns or simply did not care, and paid no further attention to them. However, the two Americans, fearing the man might want to continue the conversation, turned down a short connecting path. When they reached the end of that path they turned left and took another path. By 0200 they were clear of Rastatt and safely inside the Black Forest.

They covered nearly sixty miles during the next seven nights—an exceptional rate of march when one considers that they were making their way through the most rugged part of the Black Forest. Since leaving Rastaat they had worked their way around Baden-Baden, struggled up and down mountains that rose to thirty-five hundred feet, and crossed a half dozen rivers—some of them twice. It rained a great deal, so they were nearly always wet, and it got quite cold at night. By the seventh night both men were suffering from extreme fatigue made worse by exposure and a shortage of food.

Their fatigue, hunger, and the cold affected their thinking and caused them to take risks they might otherwise have avoided, although at the time both believed there were no alternatives. They came out of hiding long before dark on the night of 3–4 August and headed toward Neustadt, about nine miles away. Their intention was to pass through the town on the following night.

Breaking cover early was usually a mistake, but the two men were anxious to get moving. They wanted to cover as much ground as possible that night. But coming out of hiding while it was still light was not as serious a mistake as the next error they made. Instead of staying off the main roads and trails, they walked down a frequently used road that connected the small villages that dot the Black Forest. The road was fairly heavily traveled during the day. By late evening, however, there was only an occasional wagon, bicyclist, couple, or lone person to contend with—and virtually nothing moved on the road after midnight. Knowing this, Chalmers and Crowns believed there was little chance they would run into someone. It was a calculated risk, and in this instance it worked. By dawn they were just a mile outside Neustadt, and the Rhine was only a little more than twenty miles beyond that. If they could maintain the same pace they had achieved that night, they were confident they would need only two more nights to reach the river. Fatigue, hunger, and cold had led them into making two bad decisions. Unfortunately, the success—blind luck—which attended those bad decisions caused them to become even more incautious.

As night fell on the evening of the fourth, Chalmers and Crowns were faced with the task of getting around Neustadt, one of the larger towns in the Black Forest. But getting around the town was a formidable task for two men already in a weakened condition. They knew from their struggles to get around Schönwald and Furtwangen without being seen what an arduous undertaking it would be. But the thing that confirmed their decision was the knowledge that working their way around Neustadt, which is located in rugged mountain country, would be a time consuming task. Time had become critical for them, and the best way to save time was to walk right through town.

They waited until dark to start out and entered Neustadt at about 2300. Most of the houses were dark, the streets were poorly lighted, and there were very few people about. Twice they got lost after turning off the main street to avoid people who acted curious and appeared to be starting toward them. For the most part, the people on the street were men, sometimes as many as three or four, standing in doorways talking. No one seemed to pay any attention to the two ragged-looking characters hurrying down the street, intent on some errand. But someone—probably a curious Bürger and perhaps more than one—took note of the two suspicious-looking men wandering through town after midnight and reported them to the local police and military authorities.

One of the notable features of Germany during World War I was the lack of internal security. The borders were heavily guarded, and control zones extended for two or three miles back from the borders. But there were no spot identification checks, no roadblocks, and no security police inside Germany. Internal security depended on the vigilance and suspicion of the people. The authorities told them to report anything suspicious, and they did. It was a very efficient system.

The following morning, Chalmers and Crowns concealed themselves well off the road among some thick bushes under the trees and went to sleep. They were awakened by the sounds of men—many men—searching along both sides of the road. The search was orderly, disciplined, and thorough. A combined force of German infantrymen and shotgun armed civilians was combing the forest. At a little after 1000 on the fifth, two soldiers and a civilian approached the spot where the two Americans were hiding. Tired, hungry, and cold, Chalmers and Crowns stood up and extended their hands over their heads. "We were too weak to offer much resistance," Chalmers said later.[5] They had been out for nine days.

The same evening that Crowns and Chalmers surrendered, George Puryear and five others were preparing to launch the largest escape made from Friedrichfeste during the war. Puryear was teamed up with a French pilot named André Conneau, but they were not well prepared for the trek south. Their food supply was inadequate and Puryear was wearing a pair of ill fitting boots that he had gotten from a British officer. The only strong point about their preparations was the fact that Conneau had a map of southern Baden and a compass.[6]

The immediate problem facing them on the night of 5 August was the fact that Puryear was sick, and an American doctor had strongly urged him to wait until he was "better prepared." Puryear rejected the advice, telling the doctor he did not want to lose the opportunity. The fact that Puryear rejected the doctor's advice is an indication of his aggressive nature and the fact that he was often willing to throw caution to the wind. In this case, depending on where they crossed the Rhine into Switzerland, they estimated the distance they would have to cover to be between eighty and a hundred miles—a journey they estimated would require seven to fourteen days. Evading capture is a grueling experience under the best conditions, and undertaking a two week trek through rugged country when he was already weakened was a bad decision.

Puryear's problems started when he went through the window and got hung up on the supplies stuffed into his bulging pockets. The delay proved costly because he was still dangling outside the window when the sentry started back along his beat. The men inside the room frantically hauled Puryear back through the window and waited in silence. Had the sentry been alerted or had they been lucky? They were lucky. The sentry reached the end of his beat, did an about-face, passed under the window, and disappeared behind the buttress. Puryear went through the window again.

"This time I got outside and halfway down before the danger signal came again," he wrote after the war. "I couldn't get back inside this time, so I slipped on down to the ground and lay flat in the semi darkness at the base of the building. All I could hear was the pounding of my heart, and I was too scared to breathe while the guard passed within a few feet of where I lay."[7]

The sentry, probably bored and half-asleep, did not hear or see a thing. He paced the length of his beat, turned around and passed Puryear a second time without seeing him. As the sentry walked away, the American rose to his knees and was about to jump up when a squad of soldiers appeared around the other corner of the building. Puryear hit the ground and held his breath while his fellow conspirators watched in silent horror from two stories above. The squad marched past where he lay and disappeared down the dark street. Puryear released his breath, looked both ways, rose to his feet, and dashed across the street. The second man started down the rope as he dove into the shadows.

The plan was already far behind schedule when the guards changed at 2400. The escape route was designed to handle one or two men fairly easily, but five was too many. Compounding the problem was a mixup in the order that they went through the window. Instead of following Puryear out, Conneau was the last man down the rope.

It was nearly 0100 on the sixth when the French pilot finally joined his American friend in the Seidlung. The delay created a serious problem: it would start getting light at 0300 and both Puryear and Conneau were wearing their uniforms. They had to be out of Rastatt and into the forest before full daylight.

"I had on only a light uniform, no overcoat of any kind," recalled Puryear. "Conneau a good, furlined, leather flying coat which the Germans hadn't taken from him. Both of us were plainly uniformed, which of course was a dead give away if we were seen in the daytime. At night, however, my flying helmet looked enough like a German cap and our uniforms would not show clearly."[8]

André Conneau took the lead by mutual agreement. He had the map and the compass, and he claimed to be acquainted with the area through which they had to travel. As things worked out, Conneau's claim of familiarity with the area may have been overstated or else his navigation skills were weak. Whatever it was, he led them along a course that carried them steadily west as they headed south.

It started to rain at 0200 as the sky began to lighten. By then the two men were already "completely exhausted."[9] They spread Conneau's coat out on the wet ground to serve as a bed for both of them. However, the rain turned into a steady downpour that soon awakened the tired aviators. Although the coat had protected them from the water below, they had nothing to keep off the rain. They finally stood up and used the coat as a roof.[10]

Realizing they could not pass the entire day in that manner, they broke camp and resumed their march south. But Puryear's ill fitting boots were blistering his feet. In response to the increasing pain, he gritted his teeth and pressed on, even taking the lead for long periods of time. Although he "could feel the sores becoming more and more galled, they became less sensitive, and I walked on them much as I have seen a horse pull unflinchingly against a sore shoulder."[11]

Conneau said that he knew of a nearby German airfield. It was about another night's walk and on the way to Switzerland. He suggested they find the airfield and steal an airplane. Conneau may have been thinking about the training field at Freiburg. If that was the airfield he had in mind, he was more lost than they realized. Freiburg was still fifty miles away. In any event, "It being on our route, we decided that we could go by this aerodrome and see if there was any possibility of stealing a plane. We agreed not to delay long, in case of no luck, before going on foot. With this in mind as a secondary purpose, we took a small road not far from the river running south. It was then almost time to stop for the day, and being completely exhausted we were looking about for a hiding place."[12]

They had gone less than half a mile down the road when a German soldier stepped out in front of them. It was a no chance meeting. The soldier was a sentry who, upon seeing two men approaching, had stepped into the road to challenge them. But "being leg weary, sore footed, and exhausted," they simply stood there looking dumbly at the German, unable to answer.[13]

They had been free for fifty two hours and had traveled more than twenty five miles. Their fellow escapees were still out, but not for long. Within four days they were all safely tucked away in Friedrichsfeste's solitary confinement cells. Chalmers and Crowns were there, too. Although he had been recaptured, the experience provided Puryear with several valuable lessons. They were lessons he would put to use again—and soon. But first he would spend some time at the "Listening Hotel" in Karlsruhe.

The Listening Hotel, Karlsruhe

All thirteen men who took part in the Villingen escape passed through the Listening Hotel in Karlsruhe, which is located twelve miles northeast of Rastatt. Before the war it was a second-rate tourist hotel known as the Europäischer Hof. Located at Ettlinger Strasse 39, it was just a short distance from the Karlsruhe train station. The three-story hotel was "a smallish, high stooped building that bore some faint resemblance to a New York side-street boarding house."[1] The Germans used it as an interrogation center for prisoners they believed were especially valuable intelligence sources. Aviators were placed in that category almost without exception.

George Puryear told a postwar Air Service interviewer that prisoners arriving at the hotel went "up a flight of stone steps, through a narrow entrance and into a dark hallway. British prisoners were marched down the hallway to the rear of the building. The Americans were ushered into a small, dingy room on the right, near the front door."[2]

The Germans logged-in each prisoner and told him to fill out a Red Cross notification form, after which a guard searched him. However, nothing the guards found was ever taken from a prisoner, even if the items found were contraband. This laxity was intentional. The Germans wanted the prisoner to assume they were in an administrative processing center. The German officers were correct, although formal, and the enlisted guards made it clear that they knew their wards were officers.

An intelligence officer interviewed all new prisoners, asking them the standard questions about their units, where they had been based, and other military subjects. They were the same questions that had been asked over and over as the prisoners were moved rearward from the front. The difference was that the real purpose of the interviews conducted when prisoners arrived at the hotel was to assess their attitude. A prisoner with a "bad" attitude was one who resisted interrogation and was generally uncooperative. The Germans always put uncooperative prisoners in rooms by themselves, in part to isolate them from the other prisoners and in part to soften them up. But the Germans found that most prisoners were reasonably cooperative, although the prisoners usually did not realize that they were cooperating. Cooperative prisoners were placed in rooms on the second and third floors with other prisoners who spoke the same language. The number of men placed in a room varied from one to eight, the difference depending in part on each prisoner's personality and the number of prisoners to be processed. Whenever possible, men who knew each other were put together.

The floor plans and the accommodations on the second and third floors were identical. There were eight rooms on each floor. The central corridor was shaped like a capital I, with a room and a lavatory at one end and a room and a bath at the other. There were three more rooms on each side of the corridor. Guards were posted at each end of the corridor and the prisoners remained locked in their rooms except when escorted to the bathroom one prisoner at a time. The Germans permitted prisoners remaining in the hotel longer than a few days to take one hot bath a week. However, few POWs stayed there that long.[3]

Each room could sleep six or eight prisoners in double bunks. The bunks had straw-filled mattresses and two army blankets. There were also two or three chairs, a writing table, and a washstand in each room. The glass in the windows of the second- and third-floor rooms had been painted white on the outside and nailed shut. This admitted light but kept the occupants from seeing outside. It also prevented them from scraping the paint off to make a peephole.

The Germans hid microphones in every room and set up recording and monitoring stations on the ground floor. These bugging devices were primitive by today's standards and very bulky. The Germans planted two or three such devices in each room, usually hidden behind the single mirror, in-

Figure 6. The "Listening Hotel" in Karlsruhe as it appeared in 1994. The Germans used the former hotel as an interrogation center. Every room was bugged. Author's collection

side the overhead light fixture, or behind the baseboard along the wall. The furniture was then arranged so that conversations were more likely to take place near one of the hidden microphones. The idea was that the prisoners would talk among themselves and reveal useful military information to the Germans listening in on the conversations.

The most common topic of discussion was the poor quality of the German food and the lack of it. Typically, the very act of voicing a common complaint put the men at ease and they often expanded their conversations to more important matters, with an emphasis on their experiences after being captured. Such was the nature of the conversations the Germans listened to daily. For the most part there was no hard intelligence, no marvelous revelations, no revealed secrets. But they did get names and bits of rumor, gossip, and fact that helped them build a picture of the enemy, his organization, and his morale. Much of that information was passed on to intelligence officers situated closer to the front for use in their interviews of freshly captured soldiers.

Although they tried to keep officers of the same nationality together, the Germans sometimes mixed British and American officers on the basis of common language. One particularly effective method the Germans used to ferret out information was to put together a group of British officers that included one officer who was fluent in French. They would then add a French officer who spoke no English at all to the mix. The Frenchman would invariably gravitate to the French-speaking officer, who became the conduit through which the others could talk to the Frenchman. The interpreter, pleased with his center stage position, was only too willing to pass on information in both languages. The Germans accomplished the same thing by putting a lone British or American officer in a group of Frenchmen.

Perhaps because of rumors they had heard about the hotel or because they were just naturally suspicious, some prisoners hunted for and found the microphones hidden in their rooms. Typically, prisoners tore out the devices whenever they found them. Others would leave them in place and make rude comments about Kaiser Wilhelm, his family, and Germans in general. In either case, the reaction was always immediate: Guards immediately evicted prisoners who found the microphones, isolated them from the other prisoners being held in the hotel, and quickly transferred the offenders to the main camp in Karlsruhe. The Germans clearly did not want the other prisoners, especially those just arriving, to be tipped off about the presence of the bugs. But the plan did not always work. Prisoners who found the devices often left written warnings about the danger in places where future occupants would find them, such as on the back of a mirror or the bottom of a table. Occasionally warnings were scratched into the walls where prisoners thought the Germans might not find them.

The Germans tried to locate and remove such warnings but they were not always successful. After the offending prisoners were evicted from a damaged room, the Germans quickly replaced the microphones and cleaned off whatever warnings they found. But new prisoners would find warnings the Germans had overlooked, and the sequence of discovery, destruction, and eviction was repeated.

In addition to microphones, the Germans sometimes planted spies in the rooms. The spies were German soldiers who spoke French or English fluently. In the case of the Americans, the Germans had access to a large pool of Germans who had lived in the United States before the war. The spy's job was to engage the prisoners in conversation without becoming too deeply involved. He was something of a conversational shill, and while the tactic was usually successful, it did not always work. Sometimes the failures took on comic aspects.

When Edouard Isaacs arrived at the hotel, the Germans initially isolated him for two days before placing a British warrant officer in the room with him. Isaacs immediately suspected that the warrant officer was a spy because the Germans, who were terribly rank conscious, would never have placed a real warrant officer with a commissioned officer. The Germans, on their part, assumed that Americans were not at all rank conscious and believed that Isaacs would welcome his British roommate regardless of the man's rank. The Germans may have been correct in their general assumption about Americans, but not in this case. Isaacs was as rank conscious as they were. The result was that Isaacs refused to speak to the man.[4]

Meals were another tool the hotel staff used to soften up prisoners. Whether they fed a newly arrived prisoner immediately or made him go hungry—sometimes for a long period—depended on their assessment of the prisoner. They fed a prisoner or withheld his meals to get him to talk—not to a German interrogator, but to his fellow prisoners. Since the main topic of conversation was food, the hotel staff saw to it that the subject came up frequently. However, there was one thing over which the Germans had little control: the poor quality of the food they provided to the POWs. When they did feed a prisoner, the food was usually meager and of poor quality. That was not wholly intentional. By the summer of 1918, food was in short supply throughout Germany. Nevertheless, it was a fact that prisoners who had to depend on German rations starved. Because there were no Red Cross food supplies in the hotel, the most frequent complaint made by the prisoners being held there was the constant hunger they suffered. George Puryear recalled that "they made no pretense of giving us breakfast. We had nothing until noon when we were given soup and a plate of black, frost-bitten potatoes."[5]

Bernard Gallagher, an American doctor who kept a detailed diary of his wartime experiences, wrote: The Germans used Russian prisoners, enlisted men, to distribute the meals. Breakfast was usually a mug of *ersatz* coffee and nothing else, while lunch and dinner consisted of a huge bowl of soup at each meal. The soup was a thin watery broth and a few potatoes, but occasionally the Germans added a small piece of meat to the soup. The only other food the prisoners received was a fifth of a loaf of bread, which sufficed for the entire day.[6]

Nearly all the prisoners who went through the hotel assumed the Germans were deliberately trying to wear them down with confinement in the rooms and poor food. Some thought the Germans were trying to weaken them to prevent future escape attempts, others thought they were being conditioned for future interrogations. Few realized they were already undergoing a form of interrogation every time they talked to one another. And they did talk.

Bugging devices and spies were only two of the methods the Germans used to get information. The third method was direct interrogation, usually conducted a day or two after a prisoner arrived. The delay was so the intelligence officers could assess what bits of information they had already overheard, and apply that information during the interrogation. The interrogators were usually officers, although there are reports that civilians also conducted interrogations. Regardless of which method the Germans used, they always called for the prisoner when he least expected it.

The interrogation methods ranged from jovial friendliness to threats of summary execution for some alleged crime. One interrogator frequently mentioned by aviators posed as an aviation journalist who had no interest in the war but was writing a series of technical articles on general aviation topics. Another interrogator posed as a representative of the International Red Cross seeking to confirm or correct personal information for family notification.

The interrogators asked every American POW why the United States declared war on Germany. To the Americans, who were steeped in the Allied view of the war's causes, the answer to the question was self-evident: German perfidy and ruthlessness. But the question may have had more to do with getting Americans to talk than it did with trying to understand what had gone wrong because, without exception, American officers' responses were lengthy and highly detailed. For their part, the Germans were happy to keep the conversation rolling. Intelligence center and camp interrogation reports show that the apparently harmless discussions often touched on military matters and issues of morale.

Interrogators also questioned prisoners who were ill or isolated from the other prisoners. This form of interrogation was not direct. Blanchard Battle came down with influenza while he was in the hotel and spent all of his time there in the infirmary. While he was there the male nurse assigned to care for him was very solicitous and complained frequently about the war. Did Herr Leutnant think the war would be over soon? Did Herr Leutnant think that the Allies had enough men and material to end the war quickly? The nurse was terribly concerned about how much longer the war might last and full of questions about what America was doing. Battle claimed that he avoided being pulled into a conversation by saying he was too sick to answer.[7]

How long a prisoner remained in the hotel depended on two things. The first was how much information he had to give the Germans and how much of it he was giving up. Few prisoners readily gave the Germans information, but skilled interrogators were able to progressively "mine" some of the reluctant prisoners for what they knew. Sometimes this mining took as long as a week.

The other thing that determined how long a prisoner stayed in the hotel was the degree to which he unwittingly helped the Germans get information. Some men were talkers. They talked to everyone about nearly everything. Generally they were hungry for company and eager to talk to newly arrived prisoners. The talker's outgoing friendliness and apparent ease in his surroundings often caused other prisoners to open up to him. The Germans took advantage of that and used the talkers in much the same role as a casino shill. Talkers often stayed in the hotel as long as two weeks. After that they became ineffective simply because they had been there too long and new prisoners became distrustful of them.

The intelligence officers classified POWs who kept to themselves, refused to engage in conversation, or revealed nothing during interrogation as "tough nuts." Tough nuts remained in the hotel for just a day or two. George Crowns, whose stay in the hotel was less than forty-eight hours, was one of those. George Puryear, who was also labeled a tough nut, spent three days in the hotel bored to death, hungry, and anxious to be somewhere that offered a better chance of escape. He and the others would get that chance, but not right away. Their next stop was the main POW distribution camp located just seven blocks away. The Karlsruhe main camp had an unblemished record: No one ever escaped from it.

Karlsruhe Main Camp

The Karlsruhe main camp occupied the grounds of the city's zoological gardens and was directly adjacent to the former site of the city's main train station. The gardens and lawns, which had attracted strollers and had been the scene of family outings, lay entirely inside the wire. Beginning in July, 1916, hundreds of POWs trampled and destroyed the lush, carefully tended grounds. But the huge trees that the German gardeners had planted at regular intervals throughout the park remained untouched. They stood in orderly rows, their limbs stretching out to effectively shield the camp from the hot summer sun, preserving at least some of the splendor of the once glorious park. Despite their faded beauty, the park grounds contrasted sharply with the ugly security fences and roughly built prison buildings, creating a surrealistic appearance. Why had the Germans allowed such beauty to be destroyed when they could have built the camp in another, equally secure, place?

The citizens of Karlsruhe called the camp the Söhnelager (atonement camp), and although the Germans officially denied it, they had in fact built it for use as a retaliatory camp where they used POWs as human shields. The Germans believed their action was fully justified, and the camp's location adjacent to the city's former main train station and freight yard was significant.[1]

On 22 June 1916 the French mounted a five-plane bombing raid on the station and the neighboring freight yards. The target was certainly legitimate, but the French were navigating with a map of Karlsruhe printed in

1913.[2] Unbeknownst to them, a new station and freight yard had been built half a mile away shortly after the map was printed. Instead of attacking a military target, the French were about to bomb the Hagenbach Circus, whose big tent was filled to capacity with two thousand people, mostly women and children, at the time of the raid. Eighty-five children, thirty men, and five women were killed in the blink of an eye. Hundreds more were injured. The city's historian described the catastrophe as "the worst wound suffered by the city in its two hundred year history."[3]

The Germans accused the French of deliberately attacking the circus and called the bombing raid premeditated murder. Unaware that the tragedy was the unintentional result of an outdated map, the Germans retaliated by building a POW camp in the center of the city's recreation area. They fully expected the French to bomb the area again. This would ensure that French and British officers would be among the dead when they did. By the time the camp started receiving large numbers of American POWs, Karlsruhe was a regular target for Allied bombers. By then, however, the bombers were using more up-to-date maps and were hitting the new rail station and freight yard. But the prisoners knew the story behind the camp's location, and each bombing raid made them uneasy—especially the aviators, who knew how inaccurate aerial bombing could be. To them, half a mile was not all that far away.

From the air, the camp layout resembled a stubby numeral 1, with the long leg running north and south. A twelve-foot-high wooden wall topped with barbed wire that sloped inward completely enclosed the camp. Eight feet inside the wooden wall were two barbed-wire fences spaced nine feet apart. The outer fence was nine feet high and the inner fence was seven feet high. Sentries patrolled the space between the fences day and night, and the area was off limits to prisoners. Powerful lamps set on poles spaced thirty meters apart illuminated the entire perimeter at night, and guards manned posts at regular intervals in the streets surrounding the camp. The only way in or out was through the main gate on Beiertheimer Allee.

Parallel seven-foot-high wire-mesh fences set six feet apart were used to create corridors that divided the camp into five security areas. Sentries patrolled the corridors day and night, but during the day the prisoners were allowed to move freely throughout the camp by passing through gates in the corridors. The gates were closed and locked at night.

Nine roughly built wooden buildings were the only structures inside the camp. Four of the buildings housed prisoners, and a fifth was used as a combination barracks and dispensary. A long, narrow building near the main gate served as the recreation hall and reception center for incoming prisoners. The prisoners' communal bath and latrine stood in the center of the five security areas, and the administration building and the prisoners' combined canteen and mess hall occupied spaces in the largest area. The guards' barracks and latrine and the guardhouse were located inside the twelve-foot wooden wall but outside the barbed-wire fences.

Groups of officer POWs marched up Ettlinger Strasse from the Listening Hotel to the Karlsruhe main camp almost every day. The prisoners, under the watchful eyes of four privates wearing spiked helmets, walked down the middle of the street behind a German officer. Curious civilians would stop to watch the prisoner parade go by. Many prisoners viewed the walk up Ettlinger Strasse as an escape opportunity, but it was an idea they quickly discarded. Escape was impossible owing to the guards' vigilance and the people who gathered along the sidewalks to watch the "parade."

All newly arrived prisoners went immediately to the reception center. Inside the long wooden building the senior German NCO present ordered the prisoners to strip to the skin and place their clothes on a long wooden table. The Germans carefully examined every article of clothing, bending the seams, pulling the pockets inside out, and unrolling the cuffs. Shoes and boots were given special attention: guards pried off the heels and pulled out the inner soles as they searched for anything that might help a prisoner to escape.

George Puryear, recalling his experience in the reception center, described how the guards "took all equipment of any kind which you had, including my flying helmet, which left me bareheaded, in which state I remained for the balance of my imprisonment. Some of the flyers had on only flying boots. They lost them also which left them barefooted. All the money anyone had was taken up and he was given canteen money in its stead. In this manner they collected lots of maps and compasses. As for me, I never had any money nor had I been able to get a compass up to that time. My map I carried in my head."[4]

The searchers gave an equally thorough going over to all items they found in the prisoners' pockets. When Edouard Isaacs entered the camp on 19 June, a guard found a bar of soap in one of his trousers pockets and cut it into four pieces. Another searcher emptied a can of tooth powder

Figure 7. German guards march a mixed bag of officer prisoners up Ettlinger Strasse from the Listening Hotel to the Karlsruhe main camp. Such parades were a daily occurrence, but no escape attempts were ever made during this movement. Courtesy Kurt Kranich

onto a sheet of paper while a third man twisted and pulled Isaacs's tooth-brush in an effort to determine if its handle was a hidden container.[5]

When the search was completed, the newly arrived prisoners filled out Red Cross notification cards, after which the guards took them to the camp's shower house and gave them five minutes to take a hot shower. The Germans also deloused the prisoners' clothes and issued them a fresh set of underwear. Many prisoners believed that this treatment was an indication of what they could expect in the future, and to some degree it dampened their interest in escaping.

After the new arrivals had been searched and cataloged, the camp administrative officer made barracks assignments. Just as they had at the Listening Hotel, the Germans tried to keep prisoners of the same nationality together. Prior to May, 1918, when troops from the AEF first entered the battle zone, the Germans sent captured Americans to camps housing members of the armies in which they were serving. The question of how to deal with members of the U.S. armed forces first arose in Karlsruhe when Eduoard Isaacs arrived on 19 June. Captain Joseph Williamson, Blanchard

Battle's observer, arrived there on 14 June, but the Germans had simply placed him with the British officers in the camp. The presence of two American officers, and the prospect of many more, caused them to start rethinking their earlier policy.

The two Americans hardly warranted having a separate section of the camp all to themselves. However, instead of putting Isaacs with Williamson in the British section of the camp, the Germans assigned him to a French barracks—perhaps because his navy uniform was blue, as was the French uniform. More likely they did it in the belief that he did not speak French and therefore would not cause any problems. They were wrong. Isaacs spoke excellent French, liked the French much better than he did the British, and immediately joined a group that was planning to escape.

By the time Chalmers, Crowns, and Puryear arrived in the camp, there were enough Americans to warrant assigning them to their own barracks, so the camp administrative officer ordered that all of them be moved to Building 5. Building 5, like the other buildings that made up the camp, was a barnlike structure built of rough, unfinished wood. The interior was divided into eight bays with double bunks along each wall. The bunks were made of wooden slats, and each had a shavings-filled mattress and two blankets. A heavy wooden table with eight stools stood in the middle of each bay, and there was a potbellied wood-and-coal-burning stove at one end of the table. The floor was made of rough lumber.

The camp routine was the same every day. Reveille was at 0730 and lights out was at 2230. Between reveille and lights out, the only requirement was that the prisoners be present for the roll calls conducted at 0900 and 1930. The rest of the time the prisoners wandered around the camp, conversed in small groups, or simply sat and stared. Because Karlsruhe was a transient camp there were no recreational facilities, library, or other entertainment. The boredom was mind numbing.

During the day the prisoners were also allowed to visit the canteen, where poor quality wine, watered-down cider, and dried fish were available at exorbitant prices. Few prisoners wasted their precious cash at the food counter. However, despite the high prices, the canteen did a brisk business selling cooking utensils, plates, pots and pans, oilcloth, and safety matches. Business was good in part because the prisoners needed the cookware to prepare meals with the food from their Red Cross parcels. Escapees particularly prized the last two items, however, and the stock of oilcloth

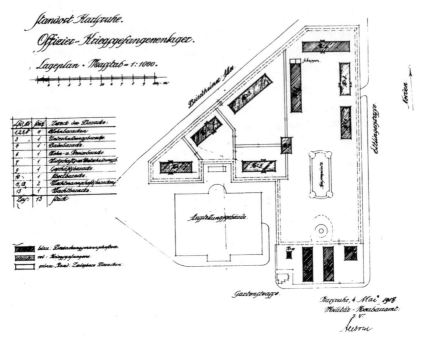

Figure 8. The layout of the Karlsruhe main camp. Courtesy Jörg Hoffmann

and matches was nearly always depleted within hours of being placed on the shelves.

The canteen also offered a photographic service, a feature in every offic-ers' camp except those designated as punishment camps. A local photog-rapher came into the camp daily from 1000 to 1400 and took souvenir pictures of the prisoners singly or in groups. The prints were ready within two days and, despite the high prices, the photographer was rarely idle.

Not all the prisoners held in Karlsruhe were content to wait for some-thing to happen. At any given time there were three or four escape plans being actively developed. Most of the schemes were never put into effect because the Germans made it a practice to transfer prisoners without prior warning. That practice, coupled with frequent searches, helped insure that no one escaped from Karlsruhe during the twenty-eight months the camp was in operation. Despite the obstacles, Isaacs and a group of British and French officers spent the time from 27 June until 3 July actively engaged in preparing an escape. Although their plan failed, Isaacs retained certain elements of the plan for later use, and he drew some important conclusions from its failure. Therefore, we need to examine the plan to gain an idea of how Isaacs's mind worked.[6]

There were sixteen people involved in the scheme, but the central character was a French pilot named Pierre DuBois. The Frenchman had been a frequent visitor to Karlsruhe before the war, attracted there by a local German girl. According to Isaacs, the girlfriend was DuBois's fiancée, although that was probably an overstatement. In any event, DuBois dreamed up a scheme that involved breaking out of the camp, running through the streets to his girlfriend's house, and hiding in her basement until things settled down. As soon as it was safe, they would come out disguised as civilians and head for the Allied lines in France.

Having established the basic outline of the plan, the next step involved figuring out a way to break out of the camp. By 3 July they had prepared an exit in the outer wall behind Building 6 at the north end of the compound, where a blind spot allowed them access to the fences without being seen. They could have the exit open in just a few minutes. The only problem would be avoiding the sentries patrolling the interior fence lines along Beiertheimer Allee and Ettlinger Strasse. It was all a matter of timing.

While they were working on the opening in the outer wall, the escapees also made "judicious use of money and French biscuits to acquire friends among the sentries." Their efforts were rewarded when one of the guards agreed to help them.[7] The guard, a nineteen-year-old Swiss who claimed to be fed up with army life, said he had run away from home the previous year and been pressed into service in the German army.

DuBois had the guard smuggle letters to his German friends in Karlsruhe and to his girlfriend. The letters included details of the escape plan and asked the friends to arrange for clothing, money, and false documents for four men. The guard returned with their replies. DuBois's friends said they would supply the required items, and the girl said her basement would be ready and stocked with food.

The escape was set for the night of 3 July and the young Swiss assured the escapees that he would be patrolling the Ettlinger Strasse beat that evening. He would time his movements to coincide with the movements of the guard on the Beiertheimer Allee beat. That meant the escapees would have seven minutes to get through the wire and through the opening in the outer wall before the guards returned to the north end of the camp.

But getting outside the compound was no guarantee the escapees would get away. Once they were outside they still had to get to DuBois's girlfriend's house. The escapees had only a vague idea of what lay outside the camp, even with the information provided by the guard. Unknown to them, the outer wall was heavily guarded. Isaacs exhibited the confidence of the uninformed when he suggested that sixteen men suddenly materializing outside the camp "would so frighten the guards that they would be unable to fire until we were safe behind a row of trees that grew only fifty yards from the camp. After that it would simply be a case of running through the city to the forest beyond."[8]

In fact, there was no cover outside the compound, just the empty Ettlinger Strasse and the buildings that lined it. Moreover, the guards could be counted on to fire at unarmed escapees, no matter how many there were. As for the simple matter of running through the city, there was more to that than he imagined. Nevertheless, despite Isaacs's overly optimistic view of how the breakout would go, there was an advantage in a large number of escapees going out at one time. The confusion caused by the sudden appearance of so many targets was sure to result in at least two or three men getting through the outer security zone. However, such a tactic works best when everyone can come through the opening at the same time. In this case the escapees would come through the hole in the wall one at a time, but in rapid succession. If they moved quickly enough, they might be able to literally inundate the guards with targets.

DuBois wrote another letter to his girlfriend on the morning of the third, this time telling her the breakout would occur at midnight that night. He gave the letter to the Swiss guard and the escapees returned to their rooms to make final preparations. At 1100 the guard, headed out the main gate in his dress uniform to deliver the letter. He did not make it. As he approached the guard shack, an officer accompanied by a sergeant and four soldiers stepped into his path. Exactly what was said is not known. What is known, however, is that the young Swiss handed the letter to the officer. The officer tore it open, read it, and ordered the guard taken away. He was never seen again.[9]

Moments after the young Swiss was led away, a company of soldiers came through the gate and deployed throughout the compound. Guards hurried through the camp ordering the prisoners to fall out for a head count. While the prisoners stood in formation, the Germans tore apart the barracks as they searched for contraband. Within a short time they had a pile of maps, compasses, civilian clothes, and sacks of hoarded food.

After the search was completed the prisoners gathered to discuss what had happened. There was little question that they had been betrayed. But by whom? That was a question they could not answer, although they all had their pet suspicions. Two things were clear to Isaacs: too many people had been involved, and the preparation and planning had gone on for too long. He resolved to limit any future escape plans to Americans, believing that foreigners, even fellow British and French POWs, were not to be trusted.

Just one day after DuBois's escape plan fell apart, Isaacs and Blanchard Battle tried to get out by hiding in a tree. Their plan was to wait until dark, crawl out on a large limb overhanging the wooden wall, and drop into the street below. German guards foiled that plan, too.

The Germans woke Isaacs up at 0600 on the sixth and told him he was being transferred. The move, although expected, left him little time to hide the escape material he had been able to collect during the previous two days. He managed to secret a homemade compass in a jar of lard and some German marks in a jar of shaving cream. He even found time to hide a map in the bottom of a cocoa tin. Unfortunately, he had to destroy the detailed maps and escape itineraries the French had given him. It was a major loss.

He put his few personal belongings in a backpack he had fashioned from an old shirt, using the sleeves as shoulder straps. Despite their paucity, his possessions were important to him—especially the jars of lard and shaving cream that held his compass and German money. When the guards turned their attention to his pack and its contents, he held his breath. One of the Germans thought the jars and cocoa tin looked suspicious and said so to the others. One guard opened the shaving cream jar and shoved a long probe inside while another guard examined the cocoa tin. The guard probing the shaving cream jar must have been careless because he missed the money stashed inside. Certain his luck would not hold a second time, Isaacs grabbed the jar of lard from the table and, "talking volubly," stirred the contents with his finger. "I explained that I was taking it to the next camp because I did not know if I should find any there—and of course it was very valuable, there being so little in Germany, etc., etc."[10]

Surprised, the guard waited until Isaacs was done, took the jar from him, and glanced inside. Seeing nothing but stirred lard, he returned the jar without comment. The map hidden in the cocoa tin also escaped discovery. Isaacs, hardly able to believe his luck, wasted no time shoving his belongings back into his pack.

He quickly dressed, picked up his pack, and went outside. There he was turned over to two guards, Unteroffizier Andreas Lindenberger and Obergefreiter August Moersch. Isaacs's luck had changed. Lindenberger and Moersch, both of whom were stupid, bad tempered, and brutal, were among the worst examples of World War I prison camp guards. The camp commander had ordered them to deliver Isaacs to the officers' camp at Villingen, located about seventy miles almost due south of Karlsruhe in the heart of the Black Forest. Although the distance by rail was less than a hundred miles, the trip took more than five hours and included a change of trains at Offenburg. From the moment he boarded the train in Karlsruhe, Isaacs was determined to jump. All he was waiting for was the right moment. But Lindenberger and Moersch remained alert throughout the four-hour leg from Karlsruhe to Offenburg. They had good reason to do so: Both men were members of the Landsturm, and it was XIV Army District policy to send guards who permitted a prisoner to escape to the front. The train change in Offenburg involved transferring to a smaller, narrow gauge mountain train. Isaacs now found himself in a car that was configured more like a streetcar than a railcar. High-backed wooden benches faced each other in pairs on either side of the aisle running down the middle of the car, forming open booths. The doors at each end opened onto platform exits; there were no doors leading to the other cars. A toilet was located at one end of the car.

Isaacs and the two Germans were seated on facing benches, with Isaacs facing the front of the train, his right shoulder against a window that was securely closed and fastened. Moersch sat on his left and Lindenberger sat on the opposite bench. Together, the two Germans, who were knee to knee, formed an effective barrier. The booth across the aisle was empty and its window was open. Isaacs planned to go through that window the moment Moersch and Lindenberger showed signs of being inattentive. But even if both Germans went to sleep, getting through the window would be no simple matter since the opening was only about thirty inches square.

As the train approached Sommerau it slowed to about ten to fifteen miles per hour. However, as it cleared the station and started down the grade into the valley below, the speed increased to nearly forty miles per hour. A few miles outside Sommerau, Lindenberger slid to the aisle end of the bench, rested his head against the high back, and went to sleep. Moersch was talking to a German soldier seated across the aisle in the booth diagonally behind them. Seeing that the way was open, Isaacs lunged out of his seat, hurled himself across the aisle, and dove headfirst through the open window, his arms folded across his chest clutching his pack in front of him. He got hung up halfway through the opening and had to shove himself away from the side of the train. He dropped straight down and hit the ground headfirst. His body crashed onto the rock ballast and steel ties, tumbled like a rag doll, and came to an abrupt and bloody halt. Meanwhile, pandemonium broke out aboard the train.

Dazed, Isaacs stood up and stumbled away from the tracks, rolling down a steep embankment into a ditch. By the time he reached the bottom, Moersch and Lindenberger had overcome their surprise, stopped the train, and were in angry pursuit. They easily caught up with him and administered one of the most savage beatings suffered by any prisoner in any war. Moersch, the more vicious of the two, broke the stock of his rifle over Isaacs's head. How they managed not to kill him is beyond explanation. Yet not only did he survive, he remained conscious throughout and after the beating.

As soon as their anger had subsided, Moersch and Lindenberger discovered they were faced with another vexing problem: The train had left them. The tracks were empty in both directions and the camp at Villingen was still five miles away. Having beaten Isaacs nearly to death, Moersch and Lindenberger now marched him at bayonet point to the POW compound's main gate.

Isaacs arrived at Villingen "limping, stumbling along, barely able to walk and bleeding profusely from the head." Moersch and Lindenberger took him into the reception building, where another guard searched him and a medical orderly bandaged his wounds. During the search the guard discovered the hidden German money and the homemade compass, but he missed the large-scale map. Following the search the Germans placed him in solitary confinement for two weeks—one for jumping from the train and one for possessing contraband. He received no further medical attention.[11]

While Isaacs was recovering in solitary confinement, most of the other men who would take part in the October escape were either in or headed toward Trausnitz Castle.

Trausnitz Castle

Trausnitz Castle is perched on the edge of a sheer cliff more than a thousand feet above the Bavarian town of Landshut. Archduke Ludwig den Kelheimer built the castle in the thirteenth century to guard the crossing on the Isar River, and his descendants strengthened the fortress in the fourteenth and fifteenth centuries. In its day, Trausnitz was virtually impregnable, and in 1918, after it had been turned into a POW camp, the castle was virtually escape-proof.[1]

The grounds, which included the castle, the surrounding buildings, and the outer wall, formed a rough quadrant when viewed from the air. The fortress was located in the quadrant's right angle and the thousand-foot cliff formed the quadrant's vertical arm. A twenty-foot-high stone wall formed the quadrant's base, and another twenty-foot-high stone wall with six towers spaced at regular intervals formed the quadrant's arc. The main entrance was a massive wood and iron door that opened into a long alley running between two twenty-foot-high walls. At the far end of the alley was a second heavy gate that opened into the castle grounds. The castle itself was separated from the grounds by a deep moat and a high, stone wall, and was accessible only across a drawbridge. At the outer end of the drawbridge spanning the moat was a three-story stone building that had previously housed the stables but had been converted to prisoners' quarters. Across the grounds from the former stables was a single-story stone building that served as the prison's storehouse and kitchen. Between those two buildings was a recently constructed wooden building that served as the prisoner reception center and hospital.

The Germans took newly arrived prisoners to the reception center to be searched. As in Karlsruhe, the guards ordered the prisoners to strip and pile all their clothes and belongings on a table. While the guards went through the prisoners' clothing, a German doctor and two medical orderlies gave each prisoner a fairly thorough medical examination. Always suspicious of their captors' motives, most prisoners believed the medical exam was a ruse. One prisoner told a postwar interviewer:

> We were immediately put through a thorough search under the camouflage of being a medical examination, which was probably the secondary purpose. We were taken one at a time into a long room, required to take off our clothes . . . and walk to another part of the room where a Hun doctor, a couple of assistants, and Mr. Capp [a German NCO] looked us over to see that we were physically OK. They also wanted to see if we had any maps or compasses hidden on our naked bodies. To examine your teeth properly they had to look under your tongue. It was a thorough examination alright. They gave us prison clothes and questioned us about our health while we dressed. They retained our uniforms for disinfecting, or so they said. But we believed they kept them to search them more closely.[2]

Despite the thorough search, one prisoner managed to retain a map of Germany that he had taped to the bottom of his left foot.[3]

Following the medical examination, the guards returned the prisoners' clothes and told them to put on only their trousers and shoes. The guards then returned the half-dressed prisoners to the medical exam room for vaccinations. Trausnitz was the only POW camp in which the Germans made a regular practice of inoculating POWs against cholera, typhus, and smallpox. The Germans may have adopted the practice because the castle had been the scene of a cholera epidemic during the Napoleonic Wars. At that time the French used Trausnitz as a prisoner camp for German officers and all the German officers held there died during the epidemic.[4]

The inoculations, administered over a period of nine days, were a painful, frightening experience. The shots were given in the chest without the

Figure 9. Trausnitz Castle in Bavaria. The Germans used the former stables (the building in the center with the white X on the roof) to house American aviators. Trausnitz was a special camp that housed only American aviators from June, 1918, until the end of the war. Its most famous occupant was James Norman Hall, coauthor of Mutiny on the Bounty. *Photo by Josef Prangl, author's collection*

usual antiseptic cleansing of the area into which the needle went, and the same needle was used on all the prisoners. Some prisoners were convinced the Germans were poisoning them. Others thought they were being injected with germs. Still others believed the Germans were using them as guinea pigs for some sort of medical experiment. Those fears were heightened by the violent reactions most of them had to the serum. Nearly every man who received the shots became violently ill within a day. Symptoms included nausea, vomiting, muscle pains, and diarrhea. Being sick was bad enough, but the misery was compounded by the fact that the toilet was nothing more than an attached, windowless outhouse. The stench in the barracks was awful, and the living conditions became almost intolerable. The inoculations were given every three days, and between shots the prisoners had little to do except feel miserable.

The POWs lived on the second and third floors of the former stables.

The guards' quarters were on the ground floor. The fourth floor was an empty and unused loft. Windows ran along all four sides of the building on the second floor. The windows varied in size and shape from three feet square to two feet wide by four feet tall. Regardless of the size and shape, each window had four vertical steel bars and four horizontal steel bars that formed a grid. The window casements were three feet thick—the thickness of the walls—and inside each window opening was a glass, multipane window that opened inward like a door.

The drawbridge spanning the dry moat and the road approaching the drawbridge were less than twelve feet from the front of the barracks. A twelve-foot-high wooden fence topped with barbed wire separated the front of the barracks from the foot of the drawbridge. The fence ran from the edge of the dry moat to a tower in the outer wall called the Folterturm. The area enclosed by this fence and the castle's stone wall constituted the prison and its grounds. Within the enclosure, eight-foot-high barbed wire fences divided the grounds into three security zones. One security zone, the prisoners' exercise area, lay directly behind the barracks. The second security zone included the reception center. The third security zone included a vegetable garden tended by German civilians. Electric lights mounted on posts set fifty feet apart illuminated the three security zones and the fences at night, and guards constantly patrolled along the fences. A line of sentries and fixed posts along the base of the outer wall provided a second layer of security.

Despite the daunting challenges posed by the fortress' seemingly impregnable security measures, Joseph Mellen, Alfred Strong, and Rowan Tucker, all members of Maj. Harry Brown's ill-fated 96th Aero Squadron, attempted to escape on 15 August.[5]

During one of his daily walks around the exercise yard, Al Strong noticed that one of the German civilians working in the garden always left his tools near the fence separating the two zones. Taking advantage of an opportune moment, he paused briefly, reached through the wire, grabbed a short steel digging tool with a wooden handle, hid it in his clothes, and then continued his walk.

It was this tool that planted the seed for escape in their minds. Together with Mellen and Tucker, Strong inspected the bars on the second-floor windows. They found that the bars, which the Germans had added in 1917, were not firmly set in the stone. The workers had simply bored holes in the casements, set the bars in the holes, and then cemented them in place. Moreover, in their haste, the workers had failed to weld the horizontal cross-bars to the vertical bars.

The prisoners' plan was to remove the bars from one of the windows, drop to the ground at night, and make their way out of the castle grounds. That was as far as their plan went. Whether intentionally or unintentionally, the Germans had built the POW camp so that the prisoners had no opportunity to study the layout of the castle grounds. So, while the escapees knew exactly how to get out of the barracks, they had no idea what they would do once they were outside. From the beginning they rejected any thought of going across the three security zones. They knew that the area immediately around the barracks was heavily guarded. Their hope was that the castle's outer walls would be less heavily guarded. As they saw the situation, the weak spot in the camp's security was the dry moat next to the barracks.

From their point of view, the moat was just a deep ditch that ran between the face of the castle and their barracks, went past the end of the wooden wall in front of the barracks, and continued on under the drawbridge. What lay beyond the drawbridge was completely unknown to them. They hoped, however, that they would find a way up and out of the moat when they reached its end. What they would do beyond that point was only wild conjecture.

Despite the lack of information about conditions outside the camp, their plan had merit. The moat did in fact extend to the castle's west wall, and there were several places beyond the drawbridge where it was easy to climb out. The problem was that once they were out of the moat they would still be inside the castle grounds and would have to scale the twenty-foot-high stone outer wall. The only other option would be to go through a gate, and that simply was not practical because the gates were heavily guarded.

Still, no one ever escaped by just thinking about it. Despite the unknowns, their plan had at least a chance for success. Buoyed by their hopes, they attacked one of the windows overlooking the moat, carefully digging out the cement that anchored the bars. They worked during the day because there was enough outside noise and activity to mask the sounds they made.

Their optimism was heightened when they freed the last bar on the third day. They knew from the beginning that they would need to fashion a rope

Figure 10. The Trausnitz Castle stables as they appeared in 1994. The building is essentially unchanged since its days as a POW camp. The windows on the floor that housed the POWs are still barred. Author's collection

long enough to reach the moat, which lay forty feet below the window. The solution was to use mattress covers, blankets, and towels that they got from their companions. No one minded giving up his mattress cover or blanket since it was only a short-term loan. Once the escapees were gone, the rope would be hauled back in, disassembled, and the materials returned to their owners.

The trio went out the window at 2300 on 15 August. Through simple luck, the window they had selected was positioned above and between two first-floor windows rather than directly over one. This meant that as they lowered themselves down, they passed between the two lower windows rather than in front of one of them. The rough stone wall afforded good footholds, and the last twelve feet sloped toward the moat. They reached the bottom without difficulty and immediately started toward the moat's far end. It was pitch black inside the moat, but the ground was fairly flat, grass covered, and free of holes. The going was easy. More important, it was noiseless. They quickly passed under the drawbridge and began to notice that the moat appeared to be getting shallower. They were right.

Figure II. A prison room window looking out into the rear yard. Although the bars may look substantial, they were easily removed. Author's collection

When they climbed out at the moat's west end they were confronted by a massive tower connected to another tower by a high stone wall. The first tower was part of the battlements and there was no entrance visible from where they were standing. The other tower housed a gate that opened onto a footpath leading down to Landshut. But the gate was well guarded. The only other way out was the main gate eighty feet in front of them, but it was even more heavily guarded. Behind them was the castle itself, and that direction offered no hope either. To the left was the prison camp, and the massive wall topped by six towers was on their right. They were trapped. Their situation was hopeless and they knew it. The only thing to do was to walk up to a guard and surrender.

The Germans reacted to the escape attempt with unusual severity. The three aviators were hustled off to the Landshut jail and placed in solitary confinement. Their original sentence of eight days was later extended to twenty-seven. They joined Toots Wardle, who was already locked up in the town jail serving what had become an extended thirty-one day sentence for jumping from a train. The Germans also locked up Major Brown and Lieutenant Battle for ten days and fifteen days respectively on charges of "suspicion."[6]

Although the trio's escape had ended in failure, it motivated George Puryear and Dusty Rhodes to join forces with four other prisoners for a new attempt.[7]

At some point in the past, someone had built a wooden wall across the eastern end of the second floor of the former stables, creating a storage room. When the German army took over the castle for use as a POW camp, the workers converting the stables into a barracks nailed the storage room door shut. The sealed door immediately caught Rhodes's attention. As far as he was concerned, doors—even those that are nailed securely shut, as was this one—are meant to open. Closer inspection revealed that the door was actually a series of panels that had been screwed to an interior frame. If the screws could be removed, so could the panels, he reasoned. Rhodes assumed that there was a barred window in the outer wall opposite the wooden partition. But Mellen, Tucker, and Strong had proven that the barracks' barred windows could easily be defeated. What Rhodes proposed to do was to loosen the door panels so that they could be removed and replaced at will. Once they gained access to the storage room behind the partition, they could work at loosening and removing the window bars in relays. When everything was ready, they would go out the window, head across the field at the eastern end of the building, and go over the wall.

It was a sound plan, though not without considerable uncertainty. Rhodes had, for example, not yet addressed the problem of getting over the twenty-foot-high outer wall. The other problem was that Landshut is about 160 miles from Switzerland—a long way for men who are poorly equipped for such a trek. But the uncertainties could be dealt with when the time came. The men immediately adopted Rhodes's plan.

Despite the almost constant presence of guards and inspecting officers, the six men made rapid progress. By 7 September they were through the door. However, instead of finding a barred window, they were confronted by another wooden partition. This second wooden wall had no door, and they correctly assumed it was built within inches of the exterior wall. The problem was twofold: They would have to cut their way through the new obstacle and they would have to do it in front of the window. But how could they locate it? One of the men finally came up with a solution. He figured that the Germans would have no reason to enter the ancient storage area, which was tightly sealed, and proposed boring peepholes in the wall at regular intervals until they found a window. They could then make their cut at that point.

The men worked feverishly behind the closed door throughout the day and into the evening until just before lights out. Puryear and three others were still suffering from the side effects of the inoculations they had received upon arrival at the camp, so the main effort fell to Rhodes and another man. Working with "ordinary Case knives," the two airmen labored to cut a man-sized hole through the inch-thick wooden wall.

On several occasions a German sergeant known as Mr. Capp stood just outside the door. The other prisoners organized a noisy crap game to cover the noise made by their companions busily scraping and sawing inside the storage room. On one occasion they taught a guard how to play craps while Rhodes was enlarging the hole through the wall just a few feet away. Another ploy was to organize a theater night, complete with noisy skits, a lot of singing, and much foot stomping. There was even a cracker-eating contest. The event was a huge success both from the point of view of the crowd and that of the men sawing away in the storage room. Just before the performance ended, Rhodes put the finishing touches on the hole. All that remained to be done was to loosen the bars in the window.

While they were preparing the escape route, the escapees gathered food, made copies of a map of Bavaria, and manufactured compasses. They agreed to form up in two-man teams as soon as they were outside the castle walls. In the meantime, new men arrived and some of the earlier prisoners were transferred away. Among the men transferred were Major Brown and Toots Wardle. Both were sent to the American camp at Villingen, and their departure started Puryear thinking:

> We learned that American officers were being sent to Villingen. We did not absolutely know this, but we had our reasons for believing it. Many more captured American fliers were coming in and we concluded that men who had finished their inoculations would be transferred from here as quickly as possible to keep the number down. The number of prisoners remained about constant at twenty-five to thirty. We believed the men would be transferred to Villingen. I knew where Villingen was located on the map; that it was only forty kilometers from the nearest point of the Swiss border. I was sure that I could in some way get out of any prison in Germany, and knew that when I escaped, I would have a hundred times better chance of reaching Switzerland from Villingen than from Landshut which was six times as far away.[8]

On 7 September Puryear asked that his name be included in the next group to go Villingen. He told the other five would-be escapees about his decision and withdrew from the group. Five days later the Germans published the names of eleven men who were to be transferred to Villingen on Friday the thirteenth. The list included Battle, Mellen, Puryear, Rhodes, Strong, Caxton Tichener, and Tucker. All of them would take part in the escape from Villingen.

Unknowingly, the Germans had blocked an escape attempt at the eleventh hour. On the day the list was published, the escape route was just a few hours away from being ready. In fact, the five who were going to use it had set 13 September as the date for their escape. However, far from being disappointed, all the men involved except Rhodes welcomed the transfer because it would position them within forty miles of the Swiss border.

Rhodes urged the others to escape that night but Puryear told him that he should be "glad to ride the train five-sixths of the way to liberty." Rhodes was not swayed.[9]

He decided to feign sickness in the hope that his name would be dropped from the list. When the group of prisoners being transferred assembled for departure, Rhodes "was the sickest looking man" Puryear had ever seen. How he managed to get that way, Puryear did not know, but he assumed Rhodes "was sick at having to abandon his plan." The ploy did not work. When Rhodes asked Mr. Capp for relief from the transfer, the German noncom told him he had to go—sick or not.

The train that left Landshut at midmorning consisted of a locomotive, a tender, and six passenger cars. The Germans reserved the first car entirely for the eleven Americans and their seven guards—an officer and six enlisted men. The other five cars were filled with a mix of soldiers and civilians.

The car in which the prisoners rode was a fourth-class coach similar in layout to a streetcar. Unlike most German railroad cars, which were divided into individual compartments, the coach was open from end to end. There was a door at each end facing the station platform but there were no connecting doors. Five pairs of facing, low-backed wooden benches lined the left side looking toward the front of the train. Each pair could seat six people. Across the aisle from the benches were five pairs of facing single seats. In all, the coach could accommodate forty people. The guards, rather than try to cluster the prisoners in one part of the car, allowed them to choose their seats. The Germans, for the most part, sat in the single seats along the right side of the car. One soldier was positioned at either end in the seat adjacent to the door.

Since they were supposed to be sick, Puryear and Rhodes lay down on the facing benches at the rear of the car. Directly across from them sat the guard who was watching the rear door. The train had hardly left the station when Rhodes told Puryear he was going to jump. Seeing that Rhodes was highly agitated, Puryear tried to calm him: "I tried to tell him that he was going to attract the guards' attention. I also told him that I wouldn't leave the train where we were if it stopped and the guards all went off chasing rabbits. We were too far from Switzerland."[10]

But Rhodes was adamant. Puryear then suggested that he at least wait until the train neared Tuttlingen, which was only about twenty miles from the Schaffhausen salient. According to Puryear: "I told him that though I was still a little sick, I was good for a couple of days in the woods, and agreed to try it with him if he would wait. I told him I had a map of that part of the country hidden in my pack, and I had a magnetized needle with which to make a compass."[11] Rhodes seemed to accept the advice and calmed down for a while.

The distance from Landshut to Villingen is a little over a hundred miles as the crow flies but it is somewhat longer by train. Despite the relatively short distance, the trip took twenty-four hours on the notoriously slow German narrow-gauge system. According to a joke that circulated before the war, a passenger, distressed by the slow progress being made by a train passing through southern Germany, went forward to the locomotive and asked the engineer if he could go any faster. "Certainly," replied the engineer, "but I have to stay with the train."[12]

Rhodes gave Puryear a push to get his attention as the train approached Ulm at around midnight on 13–14 September. They had covered a little more than half the distance to Villingen. Most of the prisoners were sleeping, or trying to, and the guards were either asleep or dozing. The guard seated across the aisle from Puryear and Rhodes was awake, but he was staring intently through the window into the dark night. Rhodes slid to the end of the bench, sprang to his feet, and bolted for the door. Too restless to wait until the train was closer to Switzerland, he jumped into the inky darkness when he was still over sixty miles from his goal. Puryear described the guards' reaction: "Instantly a rasping, hissing noise filled the car, like a dozen rattlesnakes in anger. Instantly those seven men who had looked so peaceful and quiet a moment before were as wild beasts. Each held his post with an expression in his eyes of an animal in agony. The officer moved first. He jumped to the alarm handle to stop the train, at the same time shoving his pistol into Lieutenant Battle's face, whom for some reason or another they seemed to suspect. The train stopped immediately and two of the guards went out. In a few moments they returned. He was gone."[13]

Puryear did not move during the escape or the excitement that followed. Suddenly a guard grabbed him roughly by the neck and jerked him into a sitting position. "Sick, eh?" he snarled, and shoved Puryear into the aisle. The other guards were handling the remaining prisoners equally roughly, herding them all into a single pair of benches in the middle of the car. When the remaining ten prisoners were jammed together in an area meant for six, the officer ordered them to remove their shoes, which the guards collected and carried away.

The prisoners remained under close guard throughout the rest of the trip. Six of them sat on the benches with the other four on the floor, stuffed between their knees. No one was allowed to leave his place for any reason. Puryear stared out the closed window, contemplating what Rhodes had done.

"Dusty's dash for liberty was one that anyone could admire, and we all hoped he would get through," Puryear wrote later. "I had observed his rashness, however, and had my fears of his success. I knew that to cover that hundred miles in enemy country required something more than sheer bravery and a willingness to take a chance."[14]

The Germans recaptured Rhodes seven days later.

Villingen

The Villingen POW camp was located about a kilometer west of the town of Villingen (today Villingen-Schwenningen), on the Brigach River. The camp, which was laid out east to west, occupied the former drill field and barracks of the 3d Battalion, 169th Infantry Regiment. The battalion, by 1918 a training and replacement unit, was housed in its new barracks just beyond the northwest corner of the prison compound. Although the battalion had no role in guarding the prisoners, its close proximity bolstered the camp's security.[1]

Dense woods surrounded the camp, which was located in the heart of the Black Forest. The land to the south was open and sloped gently upward toward the forest about a hundred yards away. The main compound was a 150-by-fifty-yard rectangle. A tree-lined footpath called Lorettoweg ran along the camp's south side, and a tree-lined, hard-packed dirt road called Kiels Strasse ran past the main gate along the north side of the compound. Ten one-story stone structures lined the camp's perimeter. In 1914, when the Germans turned it into a POW camp, they filled the spaces between the buildings with twelve-foot-high, barbed-wire-topped wooden fences, creating a solid, walled perimeter that surrounded the parade ground.[2]

The prisoners' barracks occupied the south and west ends of the compound, a long work shed formed the east end, and the guards' barracks and camp administration building were located on the north side. Unlike

German POW camps in World War II, the guards and camp administrative staff were housed inside the wire with the prisoners. The German section of the camp was separated from the rest of the compound by a single twelve-foot-high barbed-wire fence. The strands of the fence began at ground level and were spaced six inches apart. A sentry walked a beat along the German side of the fence day and night.

A nine-foot-high barbed-wire fence with the top angled in to keep prisoners from climbing up and over it surrounded the entire camp. Inside that fence was a seven-foot-wide ditch filled with barbed wire that lined three sides of the compound. Along the inboard side of the ditch, also on three sides of the camp, was a four-foot-high barbed-wire fence. Along the camp's north and south sides, the lower inner fence was set six feet from the outer walls of the buildings. Along those walls, the total distance from the barracks to the outer fence—including posts, wire, and the ditch— was fifteen feet. The distance was close to fifty feet at the camp's western end, where the Germans had a vegetable garden.

There was neither a barbed-wire-filled ditch nor a low inner fence at the camp's eastern end. The barrier there was formed solely by the long work shed and a wagon shed, both of which were off limits to prisoners. The Germans had built a rabbit hutch against the outer wall of the work shed. The hutch filled the space between the building and the nine-foot-high outer fence.

The entire outer perimeter was lighted at night with conventional lights strung along the outer fence, and arc lights illuminated the surrounding fields. There were twelve fixed guard posts along the outer perimeter—four on the north and south sides and two at the other ends. Each post consisted of a one-man wooden shack that provided the guard with protection from rain and snow. There were no gun towers, which were commonplace in World War II POW camps.

The camp had two entrances. The main entrance was on Kiels Strasse near the northeast corner of the compound. The other was a large wagon gate located at the western end. The vegetable garden was outside the wagon gate but inside the double-fence-and-ditch barrier. The vegetables grown there were used to feed both the guards and the prisoners. Several wooden buildings in the center of the compound contrasted sharply with the older stone buildings. Russian prisoners built them between 1914 and 1918 for use as a theater, a music room, two canteens, and an officers' mess.

A Russian-built volleyball court and two tennis courts were at the western end of the compound. A gymnastics area that included a vaulting horse, parallel bars, and a horizontal bar was set up at the compound's eastern end. The Americans added a softball diamond in June, 1918.

Two walking beats were staffed around the clock inside the compound. One guard marched back and forth along the south side of the compound in front of the prisoners' barracks, and another guard walked a post in front of the work shed at the east end. During the day the guards could see just about everything that went on in the camp. But that was not the case at night. The yard was only partially illuminated at night by ordinary electric lights attached to the various buildings. The glow from the bulbs was feeble at best, and the location and design of the wooden buildings created many dark recesses. It was possible for a prisoner to move about the yard at night if he made use of the shadows and paid attention to the guards' movements.[3]

The camp was used to house Russian officers until the spring of 1918. However, in May the United States demanded that Germany house all American prisoners in two camps—one for enlisted men and the other for officers. The problem for the Germans was deciding if the U.S. demand included Americans who had enlisted in the British and French armies, or just members of the AEF.

By June the Germans had begun to comply with the American demand. They sent American enlisted men to the POW camp at Rastatt and officers to Villingen. Neither camp was fully ready to function in the new role, but the Germans were already culling Americans from French and British camps. The first American POWs to arrive at Villingen in May and June were doctors who had been working with British units, a handful of U.S. Merchant Marine officers, and Harold Willis, the Lafayette Escadrille sergeant pilot the Germans believed was an officer.

During the early stages of converting the camp to an exclusively American prison, the U.S. POWs shared the two buildings along the south side of the compound with Russian prisoners. However, as more Americans began to arrive during the summer, and as the Germans transferred more Russians to other camps, the south side of the camp became entirely American and the Russians occupied the buildings at the west end. By mid-September there were still only seventy-seven Americans in the camp, including all thirteen of the men who took part in the October escape.

Figure 12. Villingen. Officially known as the Offizier-Gefangenenlager Villingen. Formerly the barracks of the 3d Battalion, 169th Infantry Regiment, the Germans converted the buildings and grounds into a POW camp in 1915. Until May, 1918, only Russian officers occupied the camp. The Russians built the buildings seen in the camp compound. Courtesy National Archives

The American quarters were reasonably comfortable and not yet overly crowded. Wall-to-wall wooden partitions divided each building into three twenty-five-by-thirty-foot living areas equipped with twelve triple-deck steel-frame beds, bedding, twelve chairs, and two tables.[4] A wood-and-coal-burning stove was placed in the center of each living area. The stoves provided heat during the cold nights and the prisoners also used them to cook the food that came in their Red Cross parcels.

At each end of both buildings were small, single rooms for officers with the rank of captain and above. Navy Lt. Edouard Isaacs, whose equivalent army rank was captain, occupied one of the private rooms. Doctors holding the rank of captain and Captain Williamson, Lieutenant Battle's observer, occupied the other rooms.[5] The rooms for field grade officers (majors to colonels) were equipped with a bathtub and running water. Major Harry Brown was the only U.S. field grade officer in residence, making him the only American to enjoy the luxury of a private bath.[6]

All the buildings featured large windows that were spaced regularly along the interior and exterior walls. The windows facing the perimeter fence were covered with steel mesh grills, but the windows facing the compound were not barred. The prisoners could open all the windows, even the outer windows, to admit fresh air. Each window was fitted with two glass panels that swung inward like doors and could be secured to hooks in the walls.

The Germans had done an excellent job of converting Villingen to a prison camp. Although their attention to detail created several obstacles to escape, Villingen was not escape-proof. Several Russian officers attempted to escape but none were successful. Americans began plotting escape attempts when Edouard Isaacs was released into the general population on 20 July. By mid-September—when the POWs from Landshut arrived at Villingen—Isaacs, Harold Willis, Toots Wardle, and several others had already come up with three different schemes. However, each of them was thwarted just a few hours before the plan was to have gone into effect.

The three attempts that were blocked before they could be launched served to warn the Americans that the Germans had informants in the camp. They correctly suspected that the Russian soldiers the Germans had assigned to serve as their orderlies were the informants. The Americans complained from the outset that communicating with the Russian orderlies, none of whom spoke English or French, was "difficult," and that the Russians were "frightfully unclean and most of them were diseased." They demanded American orderlies, or, if they could not get Americans, French soldiers.[7]

The Germans stalled until late October, when six U.S. soldiers at last arrived in the camp to serve as orderlies. Of course, they had good reason to stall: the Russians were their eyes inside the camp. Although the Russian peasants may not have understood English or French, they could certainly see what was going on. The guards used the information they provided to foil several escape attempts, including the first three American escape plots.[8]

But the three failures did little to dampen the enthusiasm and determination of the American prisoners. Instead, the failed attempts, coupled with a pronounced concern about internal spies, caused them to be more circumspect about who and how many people they included in their planning sessions. By late September the prisoners were actively plotting at least five escapes without coordinating their efforts.

Edouard Isaacs and Rowan Tucker were working on a plan that involved a direct assault on the wire, as were George Puryear and Caxton Tichener. Major Brown, Joseph Mellen, Al Strong, George Crowns, Blanchard Battle, and Dusty Rhodes had joined forces and were considering tunneling out. Harold Willis, Toots Wardle, and William Chalmers were working on a plan that involved going out of the camp disguised as German soldiers. However, none of the plans had advanced much beyond the talking stage at that point.[9]

There are three important elements to consider when preparing for an escape: planning the escape, personal preparation for the escape and the evasion that follows, and gathering the needed implements and performing whatever work is needed to facilitate the escape. Although seemingly sequential tasks, prisoners usually work on each at the same time. So it was at Villingen as the prisoners planned their escapes and prepared to carry out their plans. The single event in the camp's routine that played a role in each of the three elements was the daily issue of Red Cross parcels.

Around 1000 each morning the Germans posted the names of the men who were to receive parcels that day from the American Red Cross office in Bern, Switzerland. Each man was supposed to receive one parcel a week. The prisoners eagerly awaited their Red Cross parcels, in part because they served as the prisoners' primary food source and in part because they played a critical role in all of the escape plans.

The parcels came in stout wooden boxes with cardboard liners that the Germans stored in a heavily guarded warehouse in their part of the compound. Each man whose name appeared on the daily list went to the warehouse to get his parcel. However, the Germans did not issue it to him intact. Instead, they allowed each officer to select only the food he would consume that day. A member of the American camp committee working under the watchful eye of a German guard would cross off each selected item from the parcel's packing list, open the cans the officer had chosen, and empty the contents into the prisoner's dishes.[10]

In addition to the food items a man selected, the guards allowed him to carry away all the nonfood items that came in the box. The Germans then stored the remaining food in a locker with the prisoner's name on it, and the owner could return each day to draw more. The guards' main concern was that the canned food might contain contraband such as compasses, maps, files, or money. Their fears were wholly unfounded, however:

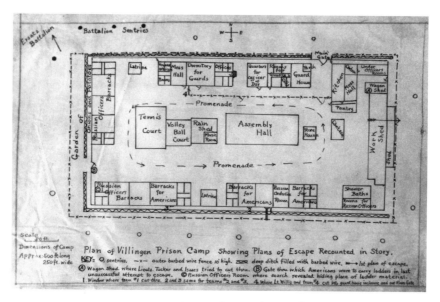

Figure 13. Drawing made by Edouard Isaacs showing the camp layout. Courtesy Isaacs Family Papers

no contraband was ever smuggled into a POW camp inside a Red Cross parcel.[11]

The camp committee also maintained a large store of emergency parcels in the warehouse. Each emergency parcel contained enough food to meet a prisoner's basic needs for about six weeks. It usually took about that long for the Red Cross to be notified of a prisoner's presence in the camp and to start sending parcels directly to him. However, it did not always work that way, and the emergency parcel supply became a critically important feature in every camp. The first personal parcel a prisoner received contained an army fatigue shirt, fresh underwear, two pairs of socks, three handkerchiefs, two towels, toilet articles, and food. After that the parcels contained mostly food, tobacco, and toilet articles.[12]

Access to Red Cross supplies greatly increased a prisoner's chance to escape. Red Cross items could be traded within the camp for escape equipment—compasses, maps, and tools. Tailors in the camp altered Red Cross–supplied uniforms to look like civilian clothes, and the escapees would hoard enough food to provide meals for a seven-day trek. The wood from the issued Red Cross boxes served a number of purposes: it could be used to shore up tunnels, to build ladders, or to create dummy walls, floors, and ceilings in the barracks. Despite close supervision by the Germans, the prisoners used their Red Cross supplies for all those things.

Men who were planning to escape found that the sundry items in the Red Cross parcels were more valuable than gold. The bar of Ivory soap, four one-ounce packages of tobacco, and half-pound can of coffee contained in each parcel made excellent bartering material. Prisoners also used these items to bribe the guards into releasing additional canned food or to obtain tools, maps, railroad timetables, and a host of other forbidden items from them. The demands of the war and the British blockade had created shortages in Germany that seriously undermined the morale and the morals of the people, including soldiers. Edouard Isaacs noted that the German guards were particularly susceptible to bribery because of their close proximity to the prisoners, who had many of the luxury items the Germans lacked. "I never tried to bribe a guard in vain," he wrote later. "In truth, it was our experience that anyone in Germany could be bribed, provided you negotiated with him when he was alone. A bit of coffee or a tin of meat would buy a guard to do almost anything, and for a cake of soap one might expect the impossible."[13]

Bars of soap were the best bargaining tool because soap had virtually vanished from the civilian market. Soap was in such short supply that the prisoners claimed that "with a bar of soap you could buy the Kaiser's daughter."[14] Tobacco, coffee, and canned food followed soap as high-value mediums of exchange. The escapees at Karlsruhe bribed the German guard who helped them with cigarettes. However, the czarist officers still in the camp proved to be the best source of contraband. Although the American POWs never fully trusted the Russians, they still felt it was safer to deal with them than with the guards. Moreover, the Russians seemed to have limitless access to anything an American needed for an escape.

The truth, however, was that some of the Russian officers were working both sides of the street. This was particularly true after the Bolshevik revolution cut the Russian prisoners adrift from any outside support. Some of the Russians practiced basic capitalism, using a part of the food they got from the Americans to trade to the Germans for contraband items. They in turn sold those items to the Americans for more food, and the circle went round again. The Russians and Germans were thus fed at Red Cross expense, and the Americans got the things they needed to facilitate their escape attempts. The downside of this arrangement was that a Russian could double his profit by offering information to the Germans. For a while at least, he could have it both ways—obtaining benefits from the Americans and privileges from the Germans. The number of double-dealers was small, but the fact that they were there made transactions a necessary but risky affair.[15]

The last two weeks in September were a period of unregulated escape activity and, with so much activity, it was impossible for the plotters to keep all their plans secret. Nevertheless, security was reasonably good. Although there were plenty of rumors, there was no specific information about what was going on. What security did exist was largely the result of the fact that the escape groups were working independently of each other. However, their paths crossed in the course of gathering supplies, and their needs conflicted with one another. Each conflict in turn made discovery more likely—a danger that was particularly evident in the wooden-slat issue.

Initially, Major Brown and his team were planning to tunnel out. It seemed much safer than risking being shot by the guards while trying to go through or over the wire. Everyone in Brown's team agreed that a tunnel was about the only way anyone was going to get outside the wire undetected. But tunneling presented several technical and logistical problems, one of which was shoring, and finding shoring material was a problem in Villingen.

Nearly every tunnel ever dug by prisoners of war was shored up with bed slats. However, with few exceptions, the beds in Villingen were iron cots with steel springs. Besides, the Germans did not allow prisoners to possess a piece of wood longer than six inches. That was the length of the firewood used in the stoves. This meant competition for the wooden slats in the few beds that had them was particularly intense. The bed slats—which were thirty inches long, four inches wide, and an inch thick—were available for use at that time because there were not enough prisoners in the camp to fill all the available beds. Not surprisingly, none of the beds equipped with wooden slats were occupied.

But Brown and his crew were not the only people who had their eye on the bed slats. Isaacs and Tucker, as well as Puryear and Tichener, needed them for ladders. Their plans were much farther along than Brown's and they had staked out the bed slats as theirs. The only remaining practical sources for wood left to Major Brown and his team were the unissued Red

Cross parcel boxes. But those were locked up in the warehouse, and the disappearance of any unissued boxes would alert the Germans. Furthermore, the doctors, who had been in the camp longer than anyone else, told them that the Russians had tried to tunnel out of Villingen on at least six occasions but that in every case the Germans discovered the tunnels before they were completed. After hearing that, they decided the problem of informers militated against any plan involving lengthy preparation and scratched the tunnel idea.[16] Rhodes and Crowns then dropped out of Brown's group, leaving Brown, Battle, Mellen, and Strong to come up with a new plan. However, Brown and his cohort never came up with a fully developed plan. As we shall see, their failure to do so resulted in a serious flaw in the grand plan.

The competition for wooden bed slats was not the only conflict. Isaacs and Tucker were competing with Willis and his crew for wire. Both teams, drawing on Willis's Eutin experience, planned to short-circuit the perimeter lights. To accomplish that, they needed three things: wire, tools with which to fashion it into chains that could be thrown over the bare wires feeding power to the lights, and a support group to do the actual short-circuiting. But the conflict between them was minimal. Willis found a ready supply of wire in the strands used to tie the barracks roof tiles in place. Moreover, he still had the pair of wire cutters he had smuggled into Villingen inside the plaster bust of Beethoven he made at Eutin. The only other area of conflict that might have become serious was in the organization of the support groups. But that never materialized.

In the meantime, Isaacs found all the wire he needed at the tennis court. Strung on posts around the court's perimeter was a single strand of a flexible wire similar to bailing wire. Tucker managed to steal over 120 feet of the wire, roll it, and deliver it to Isaacs. Unfortunately, he never told anyone how he accomplished the theft without attracting the guard's attention.[17]

Even after the Germans discovered the wire was missing, they did not ask what had happened to it. The only possible explanation for their apparent indifference is the fact that the Russians had built the tennis court at their own expense. Since the tennis court was not German property, any damage it suffered was of no concern to them.

Working at night with a pair of wire cutters he had bought from a Russian officer, Isaacs made four three-foot long chains. "I had to work with my hands under the bedclothes to avoid detection by the guards," Isaacs recalled later. "By the time I had finished the chains, my fingers were in shreds, for the wire was sharp and stiff and we had few tools."[18]

While Isaacs was manufacturing chains, Puryear and Tichener were trying to acquire civilian clothes—or something that approximated civilian clothes. At the same time, Willis and his group were hunting for something that could be made to look like German uniforms, to include rifles. Both groups were prepared to barter for Russian uniforms and tailor them to their needs. In either case, the conversions would not pass close scrutiny, although from a distance or at night they might be passable.

Although limited, there was a source of genuine civilian clothing in the camp: a group of eight U.S. Merchant Marine officers who had been prisoners aboard the commerce raider *Wolf.* They should have been sent to the civilian camp at Ruhleben outside of Berlin, but a bureaucratic error sent them to Villingen in May, 1918. There they led a sort of neither-fish-nor-fowl existence that left them dependent on the charity of the other Americans in the camp.[19]

The one problem with the clothes worn by the Merchant Marine officers was that the Germans had sewn a brown stripe into every piece they owned. The tailors did this by removing sections from the sleeves and legs of every garment and replacing them with wide, brown stripes that were clearly visible. Although the prisoners could remove the stripes, it was just one more thing added to their logistics problems.[20]

Not all of their activities conflicted, however. Some of the most important escape preparations were indistinguishable from normal camp activities. The best example, one that every man who was planning an escape took advantage of, was the parole walk. As noted earlier, parole walks were a privilege afforded to every officer in German World War I POW camps except those being punished. The privilege, viewed as a right by captured Allied officers, was never extended to enlisted prisoners.[21] Officer prisoners took these regularly scheduled walks in the surrounding countryside while accompanied by a German officer. The only requirement was that the prisoner had to promise not to try to escape while he was outside the compound. When the first Americans arrived at Villingen in May, 1918, parole walks were a daily event. As the American population grew, the schedule was changed to Mondays, Wednesdays, and Fridays. No walks were taken on rainy days.

The idea of letting prisoners roam about the countryside with only a

Figure 14. Merchant Marine officers held at Villingen were a source of civilian clothes for the men who were planning to escape. This is Capt. Robert D. Trudgett, a U.S. Merchant Marine officer who should have been confined at Ruhleben in Berlin. Author's collection

single officer escort may seem absurd, but the practice worked during World War I because it was based on the honor system—something virtually unheard of today. At that time Western society considered an officer a gentleman, and a gentleman's word was his bond. An officer going back on his word and escaping while on parole would have been guilty of a major breech of military discipline and committing a serious violation of the social code. Nevertheless, the Germans required every prisoner to sign a written agreement not to escape. This document, called a parole pass, was contained in a leather-bound booklet about the size of a passport. The officer's photograph was on the cover and inside was his written promise not to escape. The promise was written in both English and German, and the officer signed both versions. Originally the promise also included an agreement to "submit . . . to the order of the escort." But the Germans crossed out that part after an incident in which American officers refused to take orders from a German NCO.[22]

Each prisoner retained his parole pass until he left the camp to take his walk. As he passed through the gate, he surrendered it to the gate guard. If an officer broke his promise, escaped, and was recaptured, the Germans would use his signed pass as irrefutable evidence against him at the court-martial hearing. The penalty for escape while on parole could be long imprisonment or death. Knowing this, no American officer ever attempted to escape while on a parole walk.[23]

The mechanics of going on a parole walk at Villingen were simple. The officer presented himself at the gate at the scheduled time and joined the group. As the group passed through the gate in single file, each prisoner handed the guard his parole pass. The Germans thus had a headcount and a roster of the men who were outside the compound. The size of each group was limited to from ten to fifty officers—no more and no less. Until early October, the groups included a mix of Russian and American officers. The walks lasted about two hours and rarely went more than two miles from the camp. There were frequent stops along the way to view the scenery, picnic, and occasionally to enjoy a cold dip in a mountain river.

While it is true that most of the men taking the walks did so to relieve

Figure 15. German guards at the American officers' POW camp at Villingen in 1918. These men were considered unfit for duty at the front for a variety of reasons. Author's collection

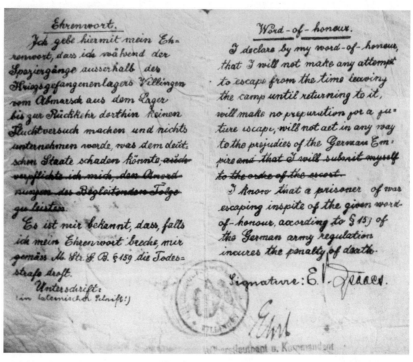

Figure 16. The inside pages of a parole pass. The English translation on the right is correct. The Americans crossed out the part that read "and that I will submit myself to the orders of the escort" because they refused to take orders from German NCOs. Each officer turned in his parole pass when he went out of the camp for his parole walk. All the escapees kept their passes with them when they escaped to protect themselves against a charge of parole violation if they were recaptured. Author's collection

the boredom, many were in fact making a reconnaissance of the area surrounding the camp. To do that properly they had to exercise some control over *where* they went and *how often* they went there. It would not do much good to take the same route every time. Whenever possible the men planning to escape urged their escort officer to show them the sights south of the camp—in the direction of Switzerland.

For many this was their first opportunity to see what the camp looked like from the outside. Could they find a weakness in the security from the outside that was not apparent from the inside? What was the country around the camp like? Was it heavily populated? Where were the best places to link up with other members of their escape team? How far did they have to run to find initial cover? Those questions and others were answered by taking advantage of the parole walks.

On 21 September Puryear and Tichener suffered a major setback to their escape preparations when the Germans suddenly placed Puryear in solitary confinement. Puryear was talking to a group of prisoners in the yard when the camp interpreter came to him and said, "I have good news for you. You're going back to jail." When Puryear asked why, the interpreter explained that he had served only five of the fourteen days he had been sentenced to after his escape from Rastatt. That meant he still had nine days left, and he was going to serve them immediately. Looking back on the experience, Puryear wrote:

> That night I was locked up again. The same night Rhodes was brought in and locked up for twenty days in a neighboring cell. The following day, though I was the only one aware of it, happened to be my twenty-fourth birthday. I shall never forget that birthday party, locked up in my cell. The boys with whom I messed were to send my meals to me. They sent them alright, but the guards mixed them up and all my meals were given to Rhodes. I fasted while he feasted. He had just been caught, however, and I suppose he needed filling up.[24]

By the time Puryear was released on the thirtieth, it was raining nearly every day. The rain brought advantages and disadvantages. All the prisoners plotting an escape wanted a dark night, and one that was overcast and rainy would be even better. There was also the added benefit that whenever it rained the guards took refuge in the one-man huts at each guard post. Being inside the huts with the rain drumming on the roofs reduced the guards' ability to hear, and the narrow doors limited their visibility. But the rain also came with cold weather, and that meant the escapees would suffer terribly from exposure.

However, the most immediate obstacle facing the men working to prepare for their escape was the lack of coordination. Although they were all aware of the other plans in a general sense, the specifics were closely guarded secrets. The danger was that someone would jump the gun, go before the others were ready, and upset everybody else's plans. The other real danger was that with so much unregulated escape activity going on, the Germans were sure to get wind of it. All that was about to change.

PART III
The Escape

The Escape, 6 October 1918

On Saturday, 5 October, before the prisoners were fully awake, a rumor swept through the camp that the remaining 150 Russians were to be transferred to another camp. The transfer was to take place on Monday the seventh. When the Russians were gone, Villingen would be an exclusively American camp.[1]

The rumor was good news to most of the Americans. They had never been on really friendly terms with the Russians, although some close relationships had developed. Many of the Americans at Villingen saw the Russians as a threat to internal camp security because so many of them were suspected of being informants. Their other main objection was the Russians's poor personal hygiene habits. Still, not everyone was pleased with the rumor.[2]

After confirming the rumor with the camp interpreter, Edouard Isaacs concluded that the sudden transfer posed a serious threat to all of the escape plans. He correctly assumed that as soon as the Russians were gone, the Germans would conduct a thorough search of the camp. The big question was when the search would take place. Instead of warning the others, Isaacs elected to make his attempt that night. He went immediately to his escape partner, Rowan Tucker, and explained the situation. Tucker agreed that it was time to go.[3]

They hastily concocted a plan that involved cutting through the wagon shed's outer wall in the northeast corner of the camp. They chose that area because there was no barbed-wire-filled ditch or low interior fence at the eastern end of the camp. Once they cut through the shed's wall, they would have only the outer fence to deal with. There were, of course, guards outside the fence, but that was the case all around the camp. They spent the entire day gathering what food they could scrounge and making their packs. At the end of the day their larder was still pretty meager, but that did not matter. This was to be a blitz effort with little planning or preparation, so they would have to travel light.

When they entered the shed at about 1830 they had with them an assortment of pocketknives and a pair of wire cutters. Both men had knapsacks they had made from old shirts, and in them were four packages of American biscuits, some sugar cubes, cocoa, and an opened can of meat. But the job of cutting through the wall proved to be much more difficult than they had expected. The problem was that the wall was made of two inch-thick hardwood boards. Cutting through the wall with pocketknives proved to be impossible in the short time they had allotted themselves. Three hours after they entered the shed they gave up and waited until lights out before making their retreat.

Isaacs had a lot on his mind as he crawled into bed that night. The Russians had already begun packing up for their Monday move, and he was certain the Germans were going to tear the camp apart. But when? Would they do it Sunday, before the Russians left? Or would they wait until Monday, after the Russians were gone? Whenever they did it, the Germans were sure to find a lot of contraband, which would have doubly bad consequences for the men who were planning to escape. Not only would they loose their precious tools and supplies, the Germans could be counted on to tighten the camp's security. Even if the Germans did not double or triple the guard, the Russians's departure would create the same effect. There were eighty American POWs in the camp, and when the Russians left the ratio of guards to prisoners would be almost one to one. At the slow rate Americans were arriving in the camp the ratio of guards to prisoners would remain low for some time. Time clearly was against them, and Isaacs and Tucker had already used up a whole day on their aborted attempt. Whatever was going to happen had to happen the next day.

It was midmorning by the time Isaacs had gathered together all the men he knew, or suspected, were planning to escape. They met in the assembly hall with lookouts posted and a play rehearsal in progress. The precautions were warranted because the Germans were already showing signs of being suspicious. Beginning on 1 October the guards made two spot checks of the prisoners' barracks each night. There were also increased spot checks of the prisoners' activity in the compound during the day.[4]

Thirteen men attended the meeting. Isaacs explained his concerns and impressed on them the need to move quickly. They all agreed but the timetable he proposed was a complete surprise: he wanted to go that night. He was convinced that anyone who did not go immediately would not have another chance. However, none of the men in the room, including Isaacs and Tucker, were ready to go, and some had not yet developed a working plan.

A lively discussion followed Isaacs's proposal for immediate action. Although George Puryear and Caxton Tichener were still short of food, Isaacs's timetable did not represent a great change as they had already planned to escape on Monday night. Puryear said they were willing to advance their plan by a day.[5]

Harold Willis next described the plan that he, Toots Wardle, and William Chalmers had developed based on his experience at Eutin. The plan involved organizing one group of prisoners to create a disturbance and another group to short circuit the camp's electrical system, extinguishing all the lights. Prior to the lights going out, Willis, Chalmers, and Wardle, disguised as German soldiers, were going to cut through the wire and enter the guards' compound. When the lights went out and the noisy distraction started, they expected the guards to pour out of their barracks and rush out the main gate to surround the camp. Their plan was to fall in with the guards as they formed up inside their compound and go out the gate with them. Willis said he believed they would go unnoticed in the darkness and confusion. Although theirs was the most complicated and completely developed plan presented that evening, it still needed work. Willis needed to make arrangements for the two support groups that would create the disturbance and short circuit the lights.[6]

Puryear and Tichener said they were going to build a ladder and use it to go out their barracks window, then as a bridge to cross the barbed-wire-filled ditch, and finally to scale the high outer fence. They had no plans for a distraction or for short circuiting the lights. Puryear said they hoped to go "over that barrier some way, get a good start on the guards and chance the rest."[7]

Major Brown, Blanchard Battle, Joseph Mellen, and Alfred Strong had

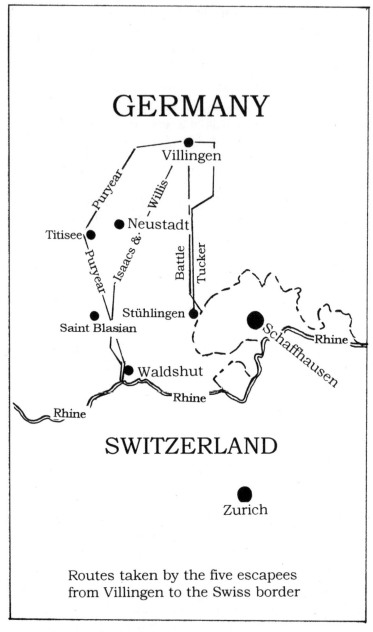

GERMANY

Villingen

Puryear

Willis

Neustadt

Titisee

Isaacs &.

Puryear

Battle

Tucker

Stühlingen

Saint Blasian

Schaffhausen

Rhine

Waldshut

Rhine

Rhine

SWITZERLAND

Zurich

Routes taken by the five escapees
from Villingen to the Swiss border

*Map 2. The routes taken by the five men who got away from the camp. Puryear,
Isaacs, and Willis stayed outside the security zone for nearly their entire trek to
the border. Battle and Tucker went right down the zone in their attempt to reach
the Schaffhausen salient. Courtesy Isaacs Family Papers*

a similar plan. They intended to go out a window in their barracks and cross the ditch on a bridge made from bed slats. Rather than attempt to scale the outer fence, however, they planned to cut through the wire. A major flaw in their plan was that Brown and his crew had not given much thought to how long it would take to accomplish that task, especially in view of the fact that they had made no provision for killing the lights.[8]

Isaacs's plan, which shared a great deal in common with Willis's, was also similar to Puryear's and Tichener's. The major difference was that Isaacs planned to build a bridge long enough to span the distance from the windowsill to the top of the outer fence. He felt that his plan would save critical time getting over the wire. He was right about that but he had overlooked a number of technical problems. Although Puryear and Tichener had a more practical plan for using a ladder, Isaacs, through the sheer force of his personality, was able to get all but Willis's team to accept his plan.

The collective plan now included two support teams, one to create a distraction and the other to short circuit the camp's lighting system, and required three ladders long enough to bridge the distance from the windows to the top of the outer fence. Willis's group would stick to its plan of going through the main gate with the guards. Isaacs also suggested some realignment in the teams.

Puryear and Tichener were planning to go out together and stay together for the run to the Rhine. Isaacs and Willis were good friends, and although they were going out by different routes, they elected to join up once they were outside. Tucker and Battle reached a similar decision, and Battle detached himself from Brown's team to join Isaacs and Tucker. That would have left Major Brown with a three man team made up entirely of men from the 96th Aero Squadron: himself, Mellen, and Strong. That was a logical grouping, but Isaacs suggested that the two loners in the group—Dusty Rhodes and George Crowns—join Brown's team. That was a bad idea because it made Brown's team too large. It would have been better to put Crowns with Brown's team and add Rhodes to the Puryear Tichener team. That way there would have been a more even distribution of escapees.

With the organizational matters out of the way, there followed a general discussion of escape routes and conditions outside. Everyone had some advice to offer since all of them had escaped at least once. The first issue was how to get to Switzerland. Everyone agreed that while trains were a good way to cover a lot of ground in a short time, few prisoners spoke German well enough to pull it off. That left travel by foot as the only practical option.

The most attractive route to an escapee on foot was to follow a course almost due south to the Schaffhausen salient, so called because Switzerland forms a bulge that protrudes into Germany at that point on the border. By following that route, an escapee could cross from Germany into Switzerland without having to swim across the Rhine. Furthermore, the border was just eighteen miles from Villingen there. But the Germans knew that, too, so the route from Villingen to the Schaffhausen salient was heavily guarded, as was the border in that area.

A much more difficult route to navigate because of the extremely rugged terrain in the region was a southwesterly line to a point just east of Waldshut. The distance to Switzerland along that route was less than forty miles, and it offered the advantage of being virtually unguarded because the Germans believed it was too rugged. However, taking that route meant that an escapee would have to swim the Rhine, a formidable undertaking even though the river was fairly narrow at that point. Furthermore, like the Schaffhausen salient, the area near Waldshut and along the river was heavily patrolled, especially the roads and bridges.

Neither Tucker nor Battle felt they were prepared to face the Rhine's frigid water, wild rapids, and vicious currents. They chose the short, dry route to Schaffhausen. Puryear and Tichener, both strong swimmers, chose the narrower river crossing at Waldshut, as did Isaacs and Willis. Major Brown's team had no uniform plan. Wardle and Chalmers seemed to favor the Schaffhausen crossing but they also talked about striking the Rhine above Freiburg and walking upriver until they found a way to cross. Major Brown, Mellen, and Strong apparently were unable to formulate a specific plan.[9]

Included in the discussion of routes were bits and pieces of information gleaned from their prior attempts to evade the Germans. Among the facts that came out during the discussion was that good shelter was almost impossible to find. Houses and outbuildings were too dangerous to use and haystacks were virtually nonexistent. Warm clothing, a rainproof poncho, and a good pair of shoes or boots that fit properly were critical. Food would always be in short supply, and an escapee could not count on finding something to eat in the fields. Food was scarce in Germany, so trying to steal food from the local inhabitants was dangerous. The best plan was to carry a five day supply, which they all agreed was about as long as the journey should take. Whatever they carried had to be light, easily prepared without fire, and nonperishable. Their choices were limited to candy, sugar cubes, and the biscuits that came in Red Cross parcels. The canned meats in the Red Cross parcels were especially good, but they were already open and would spoil quickly.

Surviving was one thing but avoiding capture was another. A threat that was even greater than exposure and hunger was the human threat. The civilian population was suspicious of strangers and, after nearly four years of war, alert for escaping prisoners. Adding to their naturally suspicious nature was the fact that civilians who captured or led the authorities to prisoners were well rewarded. On the other hand, most civilians avoided taking the initiative and asked few questions even when their suspicions were aroused. In most cases civilians simply informed the nearest policeman and let him handle the matter. The safest thing an escapee could do was avoid civilians entirely or ensure he was seen only fleetingly.

Clothing might help to avoid detection, and the more an escapee's clothing looked civilian, the better. A uniform might work if it could be made to resemble something that looked German. Civilians avoided contact with soldiers, particularly German officers, and in poor light some hats, caps, and coats might be mistaken for pieces of a German uniform. But that would only work at a distance; such a disguise would never pass close scrutiny. Most of the men in the group put little faith in Willis's plan to escape disguised as German soldiers. Another possibility was to look as Russian as possible. There were so many Russian prisoners working on farms in the area that the sight of a wandering Russian might not arouse too much suspicion.

Despite the danger of being turned in by a civilian, the real danger lay at the border. They had all heard stories about prisoners who successfully evaded capture for several days, even weeks, only to be caught as they approached the border. There were several reasons for that. In the first place, security at the borders was very tight. Physical exhaustion, hunger, and exposure dulled men's senses and some simply blundered into a sentry. Another mistake made by escapees was to let their eagerness to get across the border cloud their judgment. To be so near the goal caused many men to throw caution to the wind and bolt for the border. Those who suffered from this so-called border fever were inevitably caught and some were killed.

In many cases men approaching the border had no idea where they were. Few escapees had accurate, detailed maps of the area. Most relied on hand-drawn maps made from memory or copied from poor originals. It was not uncommon for an escapee to cross the border safely and then cross back into Germany without knowing it. Others, convinced they had safely crossed the border, reported to the first border guard they saw only to discover he was German.

In the end the escapees decided to travel in pairs. This would allow one man to sleep while the other stood guard. They also agreed to discuss each decision that had to be made along the route in order to avoid making the wrong one. It was simply a case of two heads being better than one.

Six of the men planned to go out in pairs and stay together for the run to Switzerland. Puryear and Tichener, Battle and Tucker, and Wardle and Chalmers had adopted that plan, while Isaacs and Willis, who were going out separately, would have to meet at a prearranged place. Brown, Mellen, and Strong planned to stay together once they were outside the wire since they were all from the 96th Aero Squadron. That left Crowns and Rhodes on their own. As a backup, all of the teams agreed on a meeting place in the event that they became separated.[10]

Although they were all in agreement and their plans were made, none of the men were fully prepared. Nevertheless, there was still time to make last-minute preparations if they worked fast and in unison. Isaacs suggested they organize and coordinate their activities. He and Willis would organize the support teams while seven others gathered supplies and four men collected materials with which to build the bridges. All of that had to be accomplished by 1400. From that time until lights out at 2230, they would build the bridges, loosen the window mesh, and make their final preparations. The escape was set for 2240.

The meeting broke up at that point and each group went off to carry out its assignment. It is amazing what men can accomplish in a short time, with minimum resources, and under adverse conditions. In just twelve hours the escapees melded several disparate plans into one concerted effort, gathered the required materials, and made their final preparations. While Isaacs and Willis organized the teams to create the distraction and kill the lights, the others fanned out through the camp buying food, wire cutters, maps, and compasses. Some men took wire from the roof tiles and made

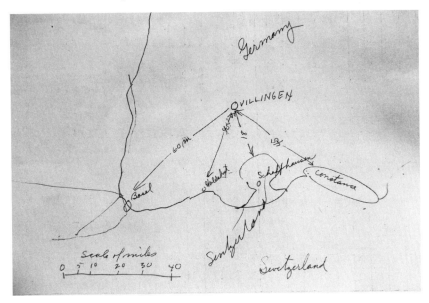

Figure 17. A rough map drawn by Edouard Isaacs showing the possible routes and distances to Switzerland. Escapees used the map when selecting their routes. Courtesy National Archives

three-foot-long chains to throw over the exposed power lines. Others pulled screws from doors, walls, and windows to build ladders. Still others gathered wood from every imaginable source. How those activities went undetected by the Germans is a mystery.

Isaacs and Willis took a big chance in asking the Russians to create the disturbance. One word from an informant would have resulted in a disaster. But Isaacs and Willis were careful to choose older men who were still loyal to the czar. They would create a distraction by rattling tin cans filled with rocks, shouting, and throwing large objects over the wire. The distraction would start at the western end of the camp the moment the lights went out. If it worked, the guards would be drawn in that direction while the escapees went over the fence on the south side of the camp and through the main gate.[11]

Six American doctors were entrusted with the mission of short-circuiting the lights. When the Germans turned off the barracks lights at 2230, the perimeter lights and the arc lights in the fields surrounding the

Figure 18. The Americans escaped through these windows in the south wall of the camp. The small, boxlike buildings outside the wire are one man guard shacks. Courtesy National Archives

camp remained on. Those were the lights that had to be killed. The wires that carried current to the security lights were made of bare copper strung fourteen feet above the ground on poles. Those wires were accessible to the prisoners in two places: the northeast and northwest corners of the compound.[12] The doctors were divided into two man teams. Since prisoners could remain in the compound after the barracks lights were turned off at 2230, there would be no problem getting into position. In any event, throwing the wire chains over the electric wires was no easy task.

By midafternoon the escapees had accomplished everything except building the bridges and cutting the window mesh. Building the bridges—or ladders, as some of the men preferred to call them—was not too difficult. However, cutting the mesh that covered the windows proved to be a major problem. The screens were made of quarter-inch-thick steel strands and securely fastened to the window frames. Each window team had a pair of heavy wire cutters, and there was one hacksaw blade available to the three teams. Unfortunately, the hacksaw blade made so much noise that it could only be used when the guard walking the yard beat was at the far end of the compound. This was frustrating because the hacksaw blade would have made short work of the bars, whereas the wire cutters were only marginally effective. It was soon obvious that cutting through the wire mesh was going to take longer than they had expected.

Compounding the problem was the fact that the mesh had to remain in place and appear undisturbed, at least to a casual inspector. Furthermore, the work was being done in broad daylight with the guards walking their beats outside and the interpreter popping in at odd times to make spot inspections. Lookouts were posted at the doors and windows to keep the escapees informed of the guards' movements. When the guard walking the yard beat approached the building all work stopped until he did an about-face and moved out of earshot. The regular interruptions got on everyone's nerves because time was running out. As each mesh strand was cut, a man would coat the shiny end with black shoe polish. The strands at the upper corners of the windows and one strand on each side were cut almost through and left in place. Those strands held the screen against the window and could be easily broken when the time came to push it out. These precautions were necessary to make the windows appear untouched to the interpreter making spot inspections every hour or two. Fortunately he did not closely examine anything. Still, his sudden appearances disrupted the work.[13]

At 1900 the Germans called for a headcount. All work stopped while the prisoners reported to the assembly hall. The escapees were convinced the Germans would search the empty barracks, with disastrous results. But the guards did not perform an inspection. As soon as they were satisfied that everyone was present, the men were dismissed.

By early evening a new technical problem had surfaced. The distance from the window to the top of the outer fence was fifteen feet, which meant that the three bridges had to be at least eighteen feet long. The extra three feet insured that both ends would be firmly in place atop the fence and on the windowsill. The problem was that the wood used to form the bridge rails was only one inch thick and two inches wide. Willis, who had been an architect before the war, pointed out that the span was "entirely unsupported." He did not think it would support the weight of a man crawling across it.[14] Unfortunately, there was no other wood to use to make the rails and no practical way to strengthen the span. Willis, however, did offer some hope. He suggested that "by putting sufficient weight on the inboard end of the bridge, and keeping our weight in the center of the bridge, that is centered between the two rails, as we crawled over, it would be balanced at least in part." He also said that they should dismantle the bridges entirely and turn the rails on edge so that they had the benefit of the two-inch thickness. Even with that change he was doubtful the bridge would hold the weight of even one man once he reached the center.[15]

Since there was no time to dismantle the bridges and start over, they decided to improvise. Several "strapping National Guardsmen from New York" were enlisted to add their weight to the inboard ends of the bridges. As the ladder bowed under the weight of the man crossing it, the two Guardsmen were to flatten the ladder's center section by forcing the inboard end downward. It was what the army called a "field expedient."[16]

While the bridge builders grappled with their engineering problem, Willis, Wardle, and Chalmers had little to do but wait and go over their plans. At 2230, when the barracks lights went out, they would cross the yard, using the buildings for cover, and duck behind the latrine in the northwest corner of the prisoners' compound. From there it was a straightforward matter of cutting through the inner fence and entering the guards' compound.

The time dragged and tension in the barracks mounted as the men hurried to complete last-minute preparations. Isaacs, Tucker, and Battle blackened their bridge with shoe polish to make it less visible and greased the undersides of the rails to make it slide more easily across the windowsill. Once they were satisfied that everything was ready, they drew straws to decide the order for crossing the bridge. Tucker drew the short straw and would go first; Battle drew the short straw and so would follow Isaacs. Ironically, Tucker was the smallest and lightest member of the team. "This was very fortunate," Isaacs wrote later, "for if the bridge broke under my weight or the weight of Battle who was the heaviest man, at least one man, Tucker, would get out."[17]

As 2230 approached, Puryear and Tichener flipped a coin to see which of them would go first. Puryear won. He then donned a recently acquired Russian cap and overcoat, "pinning up the tail to prevent it catching on the wire."[18] Tichener blackened his face and slung his knapsack around his neck. Shortly before lights out a messenger came through the room asking if everyone was ready.

The tension was painful as they waited. Willis and his team slipped out the door and disappeared into the night. Isaacs and Tucker rested the outer end of their fifty pound bridge on the window ledge and Puryear and Tichener did the same. Major Brown poked nervously at the uncut mesh strands on their window while Mellen and Strong wrestled their ladder into position.[19]

Standing on both sides of each window were two National Guard infantry officers whose job it was to knock out the mesh and bend it down. The escape teams were poised directly in front of their windows, gripping the side rails of their ladders like stretcher bearers. Directly behind them stood the men who would act as human counterweights on the ladders' inboard ends. As the minutes ticked by, six doctors, wire chains hidden beneath their coats, ambled slowly toward the compound's corners. In the Russian camp, the distraction crew gathered near the west end.

The barracks lights went out at 2230. Beyond the perimeter the arc lights bathed the area in bright light. The teams assigned to short circuit the lights signaled to the central lookout that they were in position. The central lookout watched the two inner guards move along their beats, waited until they were where he wanted them, and gave the prearranged signal. The six doctors tossed the chains upward and stepped back as they settled across the bare electrical wires, swinging gently. The lights went out—and came back on.[20] Moments later the lights went out again, except for a single, flickering bulb. Finally it went out and the camp was in nearly total darkness.[21]

As soon as the entire camp was plunged into total darkness a howling din arose from the west end of the camp. Guards shouted warnings while others ran toward the source of the noise. A whistle blew and the night was immediately filled with the sounds of screeching whistles and shouting guards. A heavy object flew over the wire and a shot was fired. The volume of gunfire rose steadily.

Inside the barracks, the National Guardsmen hurled their bodies against the window mesh. The weakened strands parted and the mesh screens folded outward. Hardly waiting for the screens to fall, the escape teams rammed their ladders through the windows, straining to reach the fence. The far end of one bridge settled onto the top of the fence. Tucker went through the window and scrambled along the bouncing bridge toward the wire. He was just halfway across when Isaacs followed and two more big officers added their weight to the inboard end. Tucker dropped over the wire as Battle went through the window.

Puryear and Tichener ran into trouble at the outset. They lost control of their bridge as the far end neared the wire and it fell to the ground. Lacking the leverage to get it back up, Puryear shoved the inboard end through the window and leaped out. Tichener was right behind him.[22]

The bridge lay on the ground, spanning the barbed-wire-filled ditch. Using the fallen bridge as a "run board," they crossed the ditch, hoisted the ladder against the wire, and started up. Things were happening fast and there was an incredible amount of noise—shouting, gunfire, and whistles. Tucker was over the wire, Isaacs was just going over, and Battle was halfway across the bridge. Puryear levered himself over the fence and dropped to the ground just as a burst of gunfire erupted to his right.[23]

Brown and his team were in even bigger trouble. Their bridge had also fallen inside the fence, but it had come down at an angle. Instead of bridging the ditch and using the bridge as a ladder to scale the fence, they wasted time trying to wrestle the bridge back onto the windowsill so they could again try to span the distance to the fence. Mellen and Strong were outside struggling with the ladder while Brown, Rhodes, and Crowns were inside shouting instructions and warnings. Time was running out.[24]

Willis and his team hid behind the latrine in the northwest corner of the prisoners' compound until the arc lights went out. As soon as it was dark, Willis stepped up to the wire separating the two compounds and cut an opening into the guards' compound. He was the first through the hole and, to his surprise, the first person in the German compound. For some reason, the off-duty guards were slow to react to the shouts, whistles, and shooting.

When Tucker dropped to the ground outside the fence, a guard who could not have been more than thirty yards away fired on him. Tucker flinched and started running, and the guard fired and missed again. Tucker later told a German court-martial board: "According to our agreement, I was supposed to wait for Lieutenant Battle at a place about fifty feet from the fence. But it seemed that the guard was running after me, so I didn't wait. I ran east along the road. After that I didn't see or meet any of my comrades."[25]

Puryear had just started up his ladder when the guard fired at Tucker.

While the guard was still occupied with Tucker, Puryear went over the fence and dropped to the ground. The guard heard the noise, turned, and yelled "Halt!" Puryear later told an Air Service interviewer that he "stood just outside the fence, the guard about fifteen feet in front of me, facing me. At an angle to my left, about halfway between us, stood a large tree. I jumped behind this tree. The guard saw me go behind it and waited."[26]

While Puryear and the guard played hide-and-seek, Isaacs landed on the ground not more that twenty feet away. He saw Tucker running and heard another shot fired from very close. There was a third German on his left who had also opened fire. Excitement and poor visibility apparently spoiled the guards' aim, because no one was hit despite the close range. Isaacs ran after Tucker, passing between two guards. Almost at once there was another shot, this one so close that he thought the muzzle flash had singed his hair. Battle came over the fence behind him and started running for the trees. There was firing all along the fence line.[27]

Puryear glanced back at the fence and saw Tichener on the ground outside the wire. The guard on the other side of the tree also saw him and yelled at him to halt. Puryear took the opportunity presented by the distraction to break cover and head up the slope.[28]

Willis, Wardle, and Chalmers were standing in the guards' compound when the barracks doors burst open and the guards inside poured out. In a flash the compound was all noise and confusion and there was heavy gunfire all around the camp. A German sergeant was shouting orders at the just-awakened guards, who were still buttoning their tunics. Many were bareheaded. Willis quickly joined up with a group of guards moving in a disorganized gaggle toward the main gate.[29] Wardle and Chalmers hesitated, lost their nerve, and quickly slipped back through the wire into the POW compound. They took no further part in the escape. Willis later told a Red Cross interviewer in Switzerland: "As we got to the main gate there was a painful pause while the gate was being unlocked. We had counted on the gates being opened right away. Instead they remained closed while the guards reported and were formed up. Fortunately the guards were so excited that they did not pay much attention to us. In fact, one nervous man kept shooting straight up into the air."[30]

Willis ran with the guards across the eastern end of the camp. Once clear of the gate area, he started "edging off," but a noncommissioned officer saw him and began shouting at him. Willis ignored the challenge. When the German shouted again, Willis threw down his dummy rifle, turned sharply to the left, and started running hard. The guards opened fire.

Isaacs, Puryear, and Battle were racing up the slope south of the camp toward the forest three hundred yards away. The gunfire was heavy, and the distinctive sound made by bullets flying past was clearly audible, as was the odd slapping sound they made when they struck the ground. Tucker was running east along the road leading to Villingen. He could still hear the shouting and firing coming from the camp, but none of the shooting was directed at him. After running several hundred yards along the road, he turned right and entered the forest. Willis was having a hard time getting up the slope. There was no doubt that the rifle fire was aimed at him. He said later that he "was much distressed by the time I got to the top of the hill. My speed wasn't very great because my heavy prison shoes were loaded with mud and each seemed as if it weighed ten pounds."[31]

With the guards' attention directed outside the camp, Wardle, Chalmers, and the doctors who had disabled the arc lights returned unchallenged to their barracks. Brown and his team gave up their attempt and Mellen and Strong climbed back into the barracks through the window.[32]

Of all the escapees, only Tichener had the bad luck to be recaptured that night. When the guard who had cornered Puryear behind the tree shouted for him to halt, Tichener halted. The range, at most thirty feet, was too close to risk being shot—and there was enough firing going on to justify that concern.[33]

While Tichener was being escorted back through the main gate under heavy guard, Isaacs, Puryear, and Battle reached the tree line on the crown of the hill. They all got there at about the same time and were relatively close together, but none of them stopped when they reached the trees, nor did any of the three exchange words. Puryear remained fairly close to Battle for some distance into the trees, and then lost track of him. Isaacs quickly separated from them and headed toward the spot where he was to meet Willis.[34]

Willis was headed toward the same location, while farther east Tucker was headed toward the place where he and Battle were to meet. Puryear in turn was hurrying to link up with Tichener. Of the three teams represented by the five men, only one pair would get together: Isaacs and Willis. They were extraordinarily lucky to have gotten outside the camp and away without being shot or captured. But that was just the start. Ahead lay formidable obstacles posed by terrain, weather, and their own unpreparedness. At least they were out and running. Luck had played a major role thus far; the question was, would it hold?

Battle

When Blanchard Battle cleared the wire he too found himself in a terribly confused situation, surrounded by German soldiers who were firing wildly. He did not see Tucker in the dark and, what with all the confusion outside the wire, he decided not to hang around and wait for him. Following his instincts, he took off at a run up the slope toward the trees intending to link up with Tucker at a hill known as the Magdalenenberg. He must have reached the landmark at about the same time as Tucker, but again they failed to make contact and Battle set his course due south toward Stühlingen. He had an excellent compass, which he had bought from a Russian, and a surprisingly good hand-drawn map to guide him. Although the map lacked detail, the important villages and towns were depicted, as were the major peaks and landmarks in the region. What made the map so useful was that the towns and villages were correctly located geographically.[1]

Battle was not really prepared for the hike south, even though he had to cover just twenty-one miles. His rations consisted almost entirely of sugar cubes and candy saved from Red Cross parcels, and he was wearing his officer's uniform, which offered little protection against the rain and autumn cold. His only assets were his boots, an excellent pair that had been handmade for him in Paris, and his youth.

Of all the escapees, Battle was the only one who managed to stick close to his planned route to Switzerland—a straight line that ran twenty-one miles through comparatively easy terrain. Given the long nights, which offered excellent concealment from prying eyes, he could reasonably expect to reach the border in three days. The major problem with the route was that it passed right through the center of the alert zone and was aimed at one of the most heavily guarded border areas in all of Germany.

Because he was so poorly outfitted with food and clothing, Battle should have been motivated to cover as much ground as possible every night. Instead he was overly cautious and moved slowly. He made a practice of scanning the ground ahead before moving forward. Sometimes he sat for an hour watching for movement to his front. The result was that by the morning of 7 October he was just four miles south of Villingen near the village of Beckhofen.

7–8 OCTOBER 1918

Battle slept well on the first day. Continuing his practice of careful recon-noitering and exercising extreme caution, he had located an ideal hiding place surrounded by thick foliage atop a low hill that offered a clear view of the country on all sides. He lay out his wet clothing in a small clearing, made himself a bed of leaves and mulch, and went to sleep. By nightfall he was well rested and his clothes were dry. He used his compass to deter-mine his line of march, selecting a prominent landmark to guide on. The walk was going to be exceptionally easy for Battle, who was passing through the same area that Isaacs and Willis had transited the night be-fore. It would be a mostly downhill walk because the ground between Beckhofen and Bruggen, located four miles away, dropped 350 feet. Even traveling cross-country he should have made better than just four miles a night. But Battle was very cautious.

He was walking across a large field at about 2200 when he was startled by the sudden appearance of two Germans. The men were standing out in the open, engaged in conversation. Battle, who had been watching the uneven ground and not looking forward, had completely missed seeing them. As he approached, the men stopped talking and looked directly at him. Battle was wearing his U.S. Army uniform with his silver pilot's wings on the left breast and his silver lieutenant's bars on his shoulders. The only badges that did not gleam were the blackened USR emblems and the par-tially blackened winged propellers worn on each side of his high collar.

He was about a hundred feet away from the two Germans when he first saw them. If he continued walking in the same direction, he would pass within about forty or fifty feet of them. It was too late to turn around and it would be stupid to run, so he continued on. As he came abreast of the Germans one of them said, "*Guten Abend.*" Battle raised his right hand shoulder high, replied, "*Abend,*" and continued walking. The bluff worked. Apparently the Germans, who were not expecting to meet an American officer, and who probably did not get a good look at Battle in the dark, assumed he was a hatless German soldier home on leave. On the other hand, maybe they thought it was best not to see anything.

Rattled by his close brush with the Germans, Battle immediately started looking for a place to hide. He found one about a quarter of a mile away that afforded both good cover and a clear view of the ground behind him. He waited there nearly three hours before he was satisfied that no one was pursuing him. By the time he emerged from his hiding place it was after midnight and raining. He pushed on for another mile or so before stopping for the day near Waldhausen. Although he had covered less ground than any of the other four that first night, he was closer to his goal because his route was more direct than those the others were following.

8–9 OCTOBER 1918

Battle spent the eighth holed up in a hollow tree just twelve miles from the Swiss border. Although cramped and a bit damp, it was a very secure hiding place and sheltered him from the rain. Nevertheless, he slept poorly. Stiff and sore, Battle left his hideout and started south as soon as the rain quit at about 1600. Ahead of him and to his left lay the fairly large town of Waldhausen. To the south was Döggingen, north of which ran a railroad track. Battle made good time going around Waldhausen and, despite the fact that it was early in the evening, he encountered no one. Feeling confident, he arrived at the railroad track around midnight.

Although Battle had been overly cautious up to that point, he now began to take greater risks. He was sure the Germans had called off their initial search, and his successful encounter with the two Germans the night before further encouraged him. The first indication of his bolder attitude came when he examined the railroad tracks. They were standard gauge, which meant it was an important rail line and that police or military guards would be in the area. Without first looking to see if the way was clear, Battle climbed the bank of the right-of-way and stepped onto the tracks.

"Halt!" The authority in the command was unmistakable. Battle shot a glance in the direction of the shout and saw a man striding toward him. For a brief moment he was undecided about what to do. Should he say something or simply bolt? The indecision passed quickly. Battle leaped down the embankment and raced into a nearby wood. As he ran through the trees he could hear more shouting behind him. It was clear that the man on the track was not alone. He ran hard for about five or six minutes until he was winded and had to stop. Head down, sucking in great draughts of air, he recovered enough to jog on.

At 0120 on 9 October 1918 the XIV Military District headquarters in Karlsruhe issued a special alert to the troops in the Waldshut, Stühlingen, and Blumberg areas. The report said that a man believed to be an escaped prisoner of war had been sighted crossing the Donau–Eschingen–Löffingen railroad line at a point near Döggingen and was last seen headed south.

9–10 OCTOBER 1918

Battle made good time on the night of 9–10 October. He had settled down after his scare the night before and began to take even more chances as he approached the border. He was losing track of time and becoming unaware of what was happening around him. Still, there was one event that night that he did not miss or forget.

As he approached Lembach, Battle saw a small shed hidden in the forest. It was nearly dawn, and the building would be a good place to spend the day since it was still raining and it offered shelter from the wet cold. When Battle opened the shed's door and stepped inside he discovered a man sleeping on the floor. Before he could back out, the man stirred, opened his eyes, and looked directly at Battle. "*Was willst Du?*" he asked. Battle stepped backward through the door and turned and ran. No one followed.

The scare forced Battle to alter his course to the west and continue walking until after dawn. He wanted to put as much distance as possible between himself and the man in the shed. When he finally stopped for the day, he was within four miles of the border.

By the morning of the tenth Battle was feeling the debilitating effects of the cold, hunger, and lack of sleep. He spent all that day shivering in a thick stand of trees, unable to sleep because of the regular military patrol activity in the area. Twice during the day he saw pairs of soldiers walking along a path less than fifty yards away. The presence of so many soldiers meant that he was very close to the border, and he watched the soldiers' movements with great interest. Ignoring the effects of hunger, cold, and fatigue, he tried to determine where the patrols came from and where they went. However, his view was too limited to reach a reliable conclusion. He knew one thing was certain, though: the presence of walking patrols meant that he was already inside the border security zone.

Battle left his hiding place well after dark and moved cautiously from tree to tree. He changed his direction to the southeast in order to pass Stühlingen on his right, using the town as a navigational reference as he moved through the forest toward the border. His goal was the Wutach River, which marked much of the border between Germany and Switzerland in that area. The Wutach was relatively narrow there, not too deep, and could be easily crossed. Nevertheless, it was not an absolutely reliable indicator of where the border lay because there were places where it was a few hundred yards beyond the river. That presented Battle with no serious concern. He just had to avoid being seen until he was well clear of it.

At around 0100 he passed through the first cordon of patrols. Ahead of him were a line of fixed posts, and beyond that line were more roving patrols. Soldiers guarded all roads leading to the river and demanded to see the special identification provided to anyone traveling within the security zone. Although Battle did not know all of those details, he had a good idea about how the security would be laid out along the river. He figured that all he had to do was remain alert, move carefully, and not make any noise.

So far, his plan and stealth techniques had worked. Just after 0300 he reached the river at a point where the forest grew to the water's edge, forming a bank about three to six feet high. Battle remained hidden in the trees studying the river, trying to decide how to enter the water without making a lot of noise. He decided to move downriver and look for a better place to ford. An hour later he was moving quietly along the water's edge, going from tree to tree, being careful where he put each foot down. He was being as silent as possible, but he still made some noise. He had already stopped moving on three occasions while foot patrols passed along the trail just a few yards away. At the same instant he saw the spot he was looking for, Battle heard a noise behind him that sent a shiver down his spine: the low, threatening growl of a dog.

He slowly looked over his shoulder and saw the dog standing ten feet away in front of a soldier whose rifle was leveled at him. The soldier said, "*Hände hoch*," and Battle, who clearly understood the phrase, quickly raised both hands over his head. He stifled the temptation to leap in the river and swim for it. He knew there was no way he could beat either the dog or the bullet that the soldier would certainly fire.

Tucker

Rowan Tucker and Blanchard Battle had planned to meet outside the wire and make their way to Switzerland together. However, the proximity and large number of guards, coupled with the heavy firing, kept Tucker from hanging around the fence. When he reached the tree line he glanced back at the camp and, not seeing his partner anywhere, went on alone. Unbeknownst to Tucker, Battle at that moment was probably not more than a hundred yards away and traveling in about the same direction.[1]

Like Battle, Tucker was poorly equipped for the journey to Switzerland. His food supply consisted solely of a box of biscuits and some meat. He had the added disadvantage of being lightly clad and poorly shod. Because of their inadequate rations, Tucker and Battle had chosen to cross into Switzerland at the Schaffhausen salient, which was closer to Villingen than the Rhine. Their goal was Stühlingen, which lay just west of the salient twenty-one miles to the south.

Although he had failed to link up with Battle, Tucker stuck to the plan they had devised because he believed that route would get him to Switzerland in three days, an estimate that was optimistic but not unrealistic. The number of miles a day an escapee can cover depends on the terrain, how populated the area is, and the time of year. The average distance most World War I escapees covered was about six or seven miles a day. In Tucker's case, the longer autumn nights allowed more time for marching, but exposure was a serious problem because it was close to the onset of Germany's hard winter season.

The terrain, a series of steep mountains ranging from two thousand to twenty-eight hundred feet high and arranged in rows like waves on the sea, did not favor a speedy advance. Adding to the difficulties were the many rivers, deep valleys, and ravines that slash through the Black Forest. Tucker had chosen a route that, although shorter, was very rugged. He also failed to take into account his generally rundown condition after being a prisoner for nearly three months. Moreover, the steady rain that was falling only made things worse. But Tucker was twenty-five years old, which contributed to his confidence in his ability to withstand the rigors of the journey.

He was also cautious. In fact, like Battle, he was too cautious. After reaching the forest he headed south to the Magdalenenberg and then turned east toward the twenty-five-hundred-foot-high Stahlberg a mile away. To reach the Stahlberg he had to cross the Brigach River. Why he chose to make the unnecessary detour toward the mountain before turning south is a mystery, because crossing the Brigach cost him a considerable amount of time and sapped his strength. He hunted for more than three hours before he finally found a place where he could wade across holding his knapsack above his head and thus keep his meager supply of crackers dry.

Once he reached the Stahlberg he turned south again, keeping the Brigach on his right. Half a mile ahead lay the village of Marbach. But between him and the village were two heavily guarded railroad tracks that he could have avoided entirely had he stayed west of the river. As it was, he lost still more time crossing the tracks since he had to avoid the patrolling sentries. It was well after 0600 when he passed Marbach and went into hiding in a wood south of town, soaked to the skin, hungry, and exhausted.

In eight hours his circuitous route had covered just over three miles, and his present position was only about two miles from the camp. At his present rate, he would reach the Swiss border in about two weeks. On the morning of the seventh he had just enough food to last two days and he was still well within the active search zone.

7–8 OCTOBER 1918

Tucker spent a quiet but largely sleepless day in the dense forest south of Marbach. Although the sun was out, little of it penetrated the thick branches overhead. Because of this, Tucker's clothes, completely soaked by the rain and the river crossing, remained sodden. The air temperature never rose above sixty degrees, and by evening he was already starting to suffer from exposure and extreme fatigue. To make matters worse, his supply of Red Cross crackers had become a soggy mess.

Tucker left his hideout after dark and set off on a course that took him south and a little west. He recrossed the Brigach at Grüningen and passed to the east of Wolterdingen. He met no one along the way and finally stopped well before dawn in the woods north of Aufen. Of the five escapees, Tucker was in the worst shape. Fatigue and hunger were rapidly sapping his strength, and being alone made him overly cautious. Furthermore, he was wasting precious time and energy by following a zigzag course toward Switzerland. In part he followed the route he did in order to bypass villages and towns, but he may also have been hoping to bump into Battle. That was not an unreasonable hope. Throughout their treks the two men were usually less than a mile apart, and at one point their paths actually crossed. But excessive caution and frequent changes in direction meant that he was moving toward his goal much too slowly. By the time he went into hiding early on the morning of eighth, he had covered only three miles and was still within about six miles of the camp.

8–9 OCTOBER 1918

Tucker spent the day in the deep forest between Wolterdingen and Aufen. Despite the heavy rain he managed to stay comparatively dry, protected by the thick limbs of the tree under which he had taken shelter. The forest floor was damp and water dripped from the trees around him, but he remained fairly comfortable huddled there against the trunk. Unfortunately, he did not sleep at all that day.

He waited until well after dark to set out on the next leg of his journey. He wanted to go south, but the presence of the twenty-seven-hundred-foot Schellenberg in that direction forced him to make a half-right turn and walk down the narrow valley between Bruggin and the mountain. Well before dawn he again went to ground, this time east of Unterbränd. Again he covered about three miles during the night, but in doing so had gotten only two miles closer to his goal.

His condition was rapidly deteriorating, and his slow progress was probably due more to the effects of the elements on his body than to overcaution. Yet despite his rundown condition and slow progress, Tucker's morale remained high. Of all the escapees, he was the only one who had not met or been seen by a German civilian, and for Tucker that was a good sign. Nonetheless, by the morning of the ninth his goal was still fourteen miles away.

9–10 OCTOBER 1918

Tucker had lost all sense of time and distance and, although not totally disoriented, he was largely unaware of the events of 9–10 October. Surprisingly, his condition, which caused him to throw caution to the wind, coupled with extraordinary luck, allowed him to make tremendous progress that night. Tucker started out traveling generally southwest in a cold, hard rain. He followed the main pedestrian road to Löffingen and then turned ninety degrees to the left to pass between Göschweiler and Reiselfingen. He said he did not meet anyone along the way, which, if true, is amazing. That footpath was heavily traveled throughout the year, and Tucker was walking on it well before midnight, a time when many civilians were still out and about. The fact that he did not recall seeing anyone illustrates the severity of his fatigue at that point.

Sometime during the night, probably after midnight, he came to the rim of the Wutach Schlucht, a chasm that he was unable to cross. He turned east and walked along the rim past Neuenburg, then around the end of the river gorge to a point somewhere near Ewattlingen or Achdorf. Despite the terrain difficulties, the morning of the tenth found Tucker in his best position since he had escaped. He was at that time only about six or seven miles from Stühlingen. If he proceeded carefully that night, he could position himself close enough to the border to make the crossing into Switzerland on the twelfth.

10–11 OCTOBER

By the morning of tenth, Tucker was beyond making any plans. All he could hope for was to make it through another day and then stumble forward. He was suffering from advanced exposure compounded by fatigue and hunger. He was unable to find anything to eat along the way, largely because he had made no real effort to do so, and all his rations were gone. All the deficiencies in his preparation could have been overcome, however, had he simply moved faster. The biggest factor working against him was the fact that he was alone. Had he and Battle made their linkup as planned, the situation would probably have been much different. As it was, by being overly cautious, Tucker extended his time in the field, which made him vulnerable to the effects of fatigue, hunger, and exposure. The slower he moved, the longer he stayed out. And the longer he stayed out, the weaker he became.

He broke out of his hiding place shortly after sundown. It was a very dark night and, in his reduced mental state, he headed off in the wrong direction, taking a road toward Bonndorf, which lay almost due west. He was approaching the town's outskirts when he saw a sign, realized his mistake, and retraced his steps until he found another sign pointing the direction to Stühlingen. Unfortunately, by the time he got back on course he was barely able to put one foot in front of the other. At some point he left the road and bedded down for the day in a stand of thick trees and underbrush somewhere between Bonndorf and Stühlingen. Despite his initial mistake and his nearly exhausted condition, Tucker had reached a point just outside the security zone along the Swiss border. He had apparently shuffled along open roads unnoticed for nearly six hours. If his luck held, he would cross the border the next night.

11–12 OCTOBER

Tucker started out on the last leg of his journey just after dark on the eleventh. He was so numbed by fatigue that he threw caution to the wind and stumbled along a heavily traveled road. He later told his German court-martial board that "my legs were too tired to permit me to go across the fields." Despite his fatigue and the fact he was on

a heavily trafficked road in a heavily guarded area, Tucker was not challenged during the early part of his walk. However, his luck finally ran out
early on the twelfth. At a point somewhere northwest of Stühlingen and
probably less than two miles from the border, a German soldier stepped
into the road ahead of him. Tucker simply stopped where he was and raised
his hands over his head.

Isaacs and Willis

It was raining hard by the time Edouard Isaacs reached the place where he and Harold Willis were to meet. They agreed to meet at the Magdalenenberg, which was located about a mile south of the camp. It was a place they had frequently visited on their parole walks and it was an easily recognized landmark. However, like Puryear and Tichener, Isaacs and Willis had made a false assumption: that they would arrive at the Magdalenenberg at about the same time. Due in part to the heavy rain that made the going slippery and slow, it took Isaacs more than an hour to reach the hill. He saw no sign of Willis when he got there and he had no way of knowing if he was the first or the second to arrive at the landmark. That presented him with a problem: Should he wait or go on?

When Isaacs reached the rendezvous point he could hear heavy firing coming from the direction of the camp. But the firing soon died down and he heard sounds that caused him to believe the Germans were calling out the three hundred recruits of the ersatz battalion. If that were true, then the Germans would soon launch their search. He decided he could not afford to wait any longer and that the best course of action was to move on along the route he and Willis had lain out.[1]

When Isaacs left the rendezvous site there were five men separately making their way toward Switzerland along three different routes. However, except for Puryear, four of the men were still relatively close to each other, the farthest distance separating them being less than half a mile. But in the darkness, the rain, and the thick forest, a few yards or a half-mile were the same as a light year. In the end, it was pure luck that brought Willis and Isaacs together.

Thus far, the only part of their plan that had worked was getting out of the camp. Behind them, and increasingly around them, there were sounds of pursuit. At around midnight Isaacs, hearing the unmistakable sounds of someone following him, ducked behind a tree. His plan was to remain hidden until whoever was behind him had gone by, after which he would move off cautiously in a different direction. The sight of a man in a raincoat and a German-style cap headed directly toward him seemed to confirm his fears. The figure looked to Isaacs like a German guard, but on closer inspection he saw that the man was not carrying a rifle. Remembering that Willis might be disguised as a German, Isaacs took a chance and identified himself by whispering, "Isaacs."[2]

The man vanished into the bushes. His reaction was not an altogether bad sign. Isaacs figured that if he were a German, he would have come after Isaacs like a raging bull. Only fugitives ducked for cover. He called out his name again, only this time more loudly.

"Willis," replied a voice in the darkness.[3]

Isaacs recalled later that he was "never before so elated over meeting a fellow human." Willis said of that moment, "We sure were delighted to meet each other."[4]

They lost no time getting underway, striking out on the cross-country route to Switzerland. Moving at a "jog-trot,"[5] the two men made surprisingly good time as the terrain initially made the going fairly easy. They had a good map and they kept to the hills, avoided roads, and bypassed villages. But they were still fairly close to the camp, well within the immediate search area. So close, in fact, that on occasion they heard trucks and saw small lamps flashing on bicycles moving through the forest along the narrow trails.

Throughout the night they followed a southwesterly course aimed at a point on the Rhine to the west of Waldshut. They had the advantage of having a commercially manufactured compass and a detailed map that covered the Black Forest as far as Saint Blasien. However, they had no map for the country beyond that point. But that was not a problem to them because they intended to strike the Alb River below Saint Blasien and then follow the Alb to the Rhine. The course they were on took them across what was essentially a twenty-eight-hundred-foot-high plateau that was by no

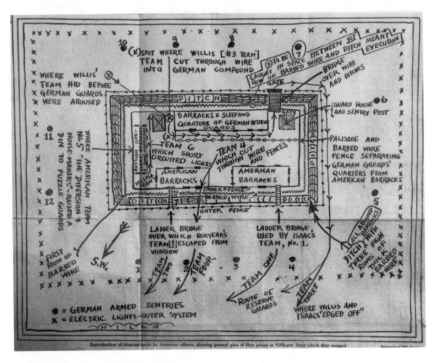

Figure 19. Harold Willis drew this diagram to illustrate how the Americans broke out of the camp. Courtesy Isaacs Family Papers

means flat, but rose and fell in two-hundred- to three-hundred-foot swells. But the going got harder when they entered a part of the Black Forest cut by gullies, crevices, and ravines, and crisscrossed with small streams. Ahead of them it was much worse.

The route they had chosen enjoyed the advantage of being a direct line to the Rhine. It also took them out of the alert zone and into country that the Germans considered impassable for escapees. They simply did not believe that poorly equipped and badly clothed escapees, living on subsistence rations, could survive the trip. And they had a good point. The area below Saint Blasien extending down to the Rhine is one of the most rugged in the Black Forest. The mountains on both sides of the Alb River are 3,350 to thirty-five hundred feet high, and the walls of the gorge through which the Alb flows are nearly vertical. As the Alb drops sharply toward the Rhine, the heights drop with it to just over a thousand feet. But the terrain is steep, broken by crevices and ravines, and cut by mountain streams.

Puryear rejected their plan because he was not equipped for the ordeal, whereas Isaacs and Willis felt they were. They were warmly dressed, had a waterproof coat, adequate food—or so they thought—and they believed they could make the trek in five or six days.[6] As with Tucker and Battle, their estimate was optimistic but not unreasonable.

Near dawn on the seventh they approached the small village of Unterbränd, about eight or nine miles southwest of Villingen. They worked their way around the town to the west and found a place on the far side where they could hide for the day. By the time they made camp they were about twenty-six miles from their goal.

7–8 OCTOBER 1918

Despite clear skies that brought a respite from the rain, Isaacs and Willis spent a restless day because the place they had picked turned out to be a poor choice. Only yards away several children were gathering firewood and nuts, and on several occasions throughout the morning it seemed that some child would stumble onto them. Both fugitives let out a sigh of relief when the youngsters packed up and left just before noon. But their troubles were not over. They were just finishing their noon meal of hard sausage and chocolate when they heard the distant baying of hounds. They could not tell with certainty from which direction the sounds came, but it sounded to them like the dogs were on the other side of Unterbränd and drawing nearer. As the baying continued, Isaacs became convinced that the dogs were following the trail they had taken during the night. Willis, though apprehensive, was less certain. He noted that it was too early in the day to break cover since there were obviously people about in the woods. The result was that they stayed where they were and spent a sleepless afternoon listening to the baying hounds. By 1600 the baying ceased and they at last felt it was safe enough to break cover and get underway.[7]

They had been walking for less than an hour and were still between Unterbränd and Weiler when they stumbled into what they called a swamp. Unbeknownst to them, half a mile to their left was Kirnbergsee, a small lake that fed a half dozen small, interconnected streams and creeks that flowed through low ground that lay directly in their path. The swampy area had places where the water was chest deep, and they had to struggle forward, making too much noise and tiring quickly. It took them more than an hour to cross the half-mile-wide swamp before they again found dry ground and the going was easier. By then, however, it was after midnight and had started to rain. The steady rain had no serious effect on them since they were already soaking wet. They also had the advantage that the stretch of ground they were crossing descended slightly so that the wet grass and muddy ground, which would have made an uphill climb difficult, posed no significant problem.

The deeper they pushed into the Black Forest, the more surprised they were at how densely populated it was. The people posed a much more serious problem to them than did the rain. They frequently came upon small villages of ten to twenty houses surrounded by farmland. Furthermore, the distance between the villages, usually just two or three miles, meant that the farms occupied nearly every clearing in the forest. Each of those small villages represented an obstacle that they had to go around. However, there was an important benefit as well. They were finding that the conventional wisdom that food was hard to find was inaccurate. The fields surrounding the small villages proved to be a regular source of turnips, potatoes, and cabbage. As a result, Isaacs and Willis were never short of something to eat.

Continuing on a southwesterly course they passed Röthenbach and came to a deep gorge called the Wutach Schlucht, through which ran the Wutach River. Unable to cross the chasm, they stopped for the day and made camp. Their plan was to go west along the rim of the gorge until they could find a place to cross, then continue southwest toward the Alb. Isaacs and Willis had chosen the most difficult route to follow because there was less likelihood of running into German soldiers. They also reasoned that the citizens in that part of the Black Forest would be less suspicious of strangers.[8] Their first assumption was right but they were way off base on the second.

Even more important was the fact that they were about to enter the most difficult part of their journey. The route ahead of them was much steeper and more rugged, and they were already tired. When they stopped on the lip of the Wutach Schlucht on the morning of the eighth, they were about fourteen miles from Villingen. Seven miles a night was a good pace for any escapee to achieve. If they could just keep it up they might reach Switzerland by the eleventh.

Isaacs and Willis spent the next day huddled under Willis's raincoat. They again went without sleep because of the cold and the presence of people working in the woods nearby. That there were people anywhere near them had come as an unpleasant surprise. Since midnight they had been traveling through an area that was surprisingly devoid of houses or farms. They had not even encountered a hunter's cabin. Moreover, according to their estimate, they were at least four miles northeast of the next town, Grünwald. Believing they were in an uninhabited area, they had placed a higher premium on finding a dry spot than one that was a secure place to hide. Now there were people less than a hundred yards away. The two Americans figured the people were probably gathering firewood or mushrooms. Isaacs wanted to break camp and slip away to the west, but Willis again argued against the idea. The group showed no signs of moving toward them, and Willis was concerned that any movement they made would attract attention. The Germans remained in the area until after 1400, but even after they left Isaacs and Willis were unable to relax. They spent an uncomfortable time waiting for nightfall. When it finally stopped raining at about 1600 they started out despite the fact that it was not quite dark.

Isaacs and Willis were nearing the limit of their detailed map. They had moved west along the lip of the Wutach Schlucht hoping to find a place to cross. However, by the time they reached the place where the Haslach and the Gutach Rivers joined the Wutach, it was apparent they could not continue the search. The main obstacle was a railroad that approached the gorge from the north and then turned west, running along its rim. If they continued west they would have to walk along the tracks and go through several tunnels, which would almost certainly have led them right into the arms of an army patrol. They had no choice but to climb down the cliff to the chasm's narrow floor.

The task turned out to be less difficult than it had appeared. The climb down was relatively easy, although the climb back up the far side was a tiring experience. Nevertheless, after they had gained the south side, their progress increased until they ran into a heavily populated area that they tried to go around. In doing so, they became temporarily lost. Willis recalled their attempt to find a way around the houses: "We struck a road which ended in the woods. We tried to find a continuation of the road and walked around in a circle. Finally we retraced our steps. We lost two hours that night. Toward dawn we passed a fine vegetable garden belonging to an old monastery. We took two fine heads of cabbage which were certainly most welcome."[9]

Early on the morning of the ninth they reached a point near the eastern end of a lake called the Schluchsee and went to ground. They were slightly north of the Saint Blasien–Häusern line, sixteen miles from the Rhine.

9–10 OCTOBER 1918

That Isaacs and Willis were nearing the end of their endurance is evident in their postwar writings and interviews about their escape. Their accounts lack detail and are often confused regarding events from the ninth on. They were both in the physical and mental condition that proved to be the undoing of so many escapees who were near freedom. Their judgment was diminished and they were getting careless. There was also the fact that they were very nearly within reach of their goal by the morning of the ninth. As they reached the end of their endurance, their close proximity to freedom caused them to become impatient. They both had a bad case of border fever.

It rained all day on the ninth and the temperature dropped to below forty degrees. It was so cold and wet that the two Americans, unable to rest or sleep, decided to start early just to keep warm. Their goal that night was the Alb River, which they planned to reach by passing between Häusern and the resort town of Saint Blasien. Once on the Alb, they would turn south and follow it to the Rhine.

Because of the distance they had to cover and the bad terrain they would have to cross, coupled with the fact that they were exhausted and cold, they decided to walk along a road in order to make better time and conserve their strength. They justified their decision by saying that the road was not really a road; it was just a path through the forest. Although it was obvious people used the path regularly, they further justified their decision by saying that the pouring rain would keep travelers indoors. Their expectations seemed to be met during the first several hours of their march. They were making very good time along the path, and they even regained some of their lost strength. Better still, they were warmer than they had been all day. But all that changed when they nearly collided with a German walking in the opposite direction. The fact that they did not see him coming illustrates both how tired they were and how dark it was. They would certainly have collided had they all continued walking, but the German gave way, stepping to his right to pass by them. They did not exchange a word. However, after he passed, the German visibly increased his pace and disappeared.

Isaacs and Willis hoped that the man was either uninterested in them or had been wary of speaking to two scruffy-looking strangers on a dark night on a deserted road. Yet they dared not overlook the incident. They had to decide whether to either continue using the path or strike out cross-country. Their desire to continue along the path was nearly overpowering since using it made walking much less tiring and allowed them to make vastly better progress. But their better judgment prevailed and they headed back into the forest. It was a sound decision and shows that, although badly fatigued, they were still capable of making one. The fact that they were traveling together undoubtedly contributed to their continued ability to show good judgment. They did not know it, but the man they had passed did report the incident to the police at Faulenfürst.

Despite being sound, the decision to revert to cross-country travel presented them with big problems. They were now in a part of the country where the terrain was very rough. Their progress slowed and their strength ebbed. There was no level ground, just one steep climb followed by a steep descent, followed by another steep climb. The mountains seemed to be getting higher and the valleys deeper. They had also gone beyond the limits of their map, which meant they were farther south than they thought they were.

"We struck another deep mountain valley and passed many houses with lights in them," recalled Isaacs. "During the early morning hours as we were going west instead of south . . . we struck a road that ended in the woods. We tried to find a continuation of the road and walked in a circle. Finally we retraced our steps. We lost two hours that night. . . . We now struck the most mountainous part of the Schwartzwald, and were not far from St. Blasien."[10]

While they were slightly farther south than they had intended, their navigation had been good. They were now below the resort town and on a cliff above the Alb close to the spot for which they had been aiming. They spent nearly three hours making their way down the cliff to the river, a drop of about two hundred feet, later describing the descent as "slow and nerve racking." Standing at the bottom of the gorge looking up, Isaacs commented, "It seemed impossible that we had been able to cling to the vertical wall of rock and lower ourselves down."

According to their plan, they were to remain in the gorge and follow the river down to the Rhine. That plan was based on the belief that the Alb gorge between Saint Blasien and the Rhine was essentially an unpopulated alley to freedom. It had never occurred to them that a place so inaccessible would be inhabited. In fact, the west bank of the Alb was heavily populated. Isaacs noted that they "soon came to logging camps, summer hotels, electric power plants and breweries all built between the west bank of the river and the high cliff. After walking over front porches, under driveways and through barns, we decided it was too risky."[11]

They obviously dared not remain in the gorge after daylight since there was no place to hide with so many people around. They had no choice but to scale the high cliff along the west bank and make their way to the Rhine along the plateau. They managed to scale the cliff despite being bone tired and the fact that it was dark and raining. Once they were on they plateau they went into hiding just as dawn broke.

It did not rain during the day on the tenth, but the temperature dropped to near freezing. Isaacs and Willis spent the daylight hours huddled together with Willis's raincoat thrown over them like a blanket, trying to stay warm. It was a losing battle. The cold made it almost impossible to sleep even though both men were suffering from extreme fatigue. With nothing else to occupy their time, they considered their plans for the coming night.

The map they had was useless because they were beyond its limit and they were forced to scrap their original plan to follow the Alb down to the Rhine because the area was so heavily populated and there was no place to hide in the narrow gorge. Nevertheless, they were confident that by keeping to the valley's rim they could still follow the river to the Rhine. The only problem they could envision at that point was getting down to the river from the plateau.

The two escapees made little progress on the night of 10–11 October. Their plan to continue south across the high plateau had proved to be unworkable. Willis told a postwar interviewer that the region was full of "deep and narrow valleys. Along the bottom of the valleys are rows of houses, and on the plateau are other villages running along the crest. To have walked in the valleys would have meant much less work . . . but we could not chance detection. We also avoided the high plateaus for the same reason, and kept halfway up the slopes of the mountains where the going was terribly difficult, but safer."[12]

Since they were without a map they often became lost for hours, and at one point found themselves in a canyon from which there was no way out. Their only recourse was to double back. Their progress was slowed further by the many swiftly running rivers and streams that cut through the area. Isaacs later said, "Every few hundred yards was a mountain torrent, and every torrent meant a difficult gorge to negotiate."[13]

They were also encountering more civilians than at any other time during their journey south. "Several times we met people," Isaacs wrote later. "Once we came across a couple who sprang up in alarm and ran at top speed when they saw us. One man grunted as we passed, but others went by without speaking, which is unusual in the rural districts of Germany."[14]

The frequent encounters had a dual effect on them. On one hand, they were justifiably concerned that someone was going to report them. On the other hand, they noticed a surprising level of indifference among the civilians they encountered. As a result, they came to the conclusion that they could move more openly and therefore more quickly toward the Rhine. At the moment, however, it was the lack of a good map and the difficulty of the terrain rather than the presence of civilians that was slowing them down. By daybreak on the eleventh they thus had advanced their position by less than three miles.

11–12 OCTOBER 1918

Isaacs and Willis were "in a heavy sleep" in a small clearing nine miles from the Rhine on the morning of the eleventh, blissfully unaware that a team of woodcutters had set up operations near their campsite. The noise the woodcutters made was not what awakened Isaacs, however. "I sat up and to my horror discovered that Willis was delirious. He was babbling incoherently and seemed to have a high fever. I soothed him as well as I could, and in a few hours he was back to normal."[15]

Isaacs's immediate concern was that Willis's babbling would attract the woodcutters, who were less than thirty yards away. But they were making too much noise to be able to hear Willis. A much more serious concern was the cause of Willis's babbling. Both men were under enormous strain and suffering from extreme fatigue. A visible symptom was the fact that during the last five days, Willis's hair had turned completely white. Adding to their problems was the fact that Isaacs had not fully recovered from the beating he received after his earlier escape attempt.

The woodcutters finished their work and were gone by midmorning. The sun came out, the sky became almost cloudless, and the temperature began to rise. Their day camp was in a small clearing surrounded by thick brush and trees, and both men took advantage of the good weather to strip and hang their clothing on bushes to dry. Isaacs was lying in the open asleep and Willis was awake, sitting with his back to a tree, when a German suddenly stepped into the clearing. The man, a civilian, stopped not more than six feet from Isaacs, looked directly at him, said nothing, and left the clearing by the same way he had entered.

Stunned, Willis woke his friend and told him what had happened. What should they do? After some discussion they agreed it was too early to get underway, especially with the weather so good. A horde of people surely would be out on a day like this. They decided to stay where they were but remain awake and on guard. If they saw anyone coming their way, they would run. The remainder of the day was uneventful. Apparently the civilian had thought nothing of finding a sleeping man in the forest. When night fell they started toward the Rhine on what proved to be the last leg of their journey.

There were now only two escapees trying to reach the river, and they were nearly as tired as Tucker had been. The absence of details about the night of 11–12 October in their narratives is an indicator of just how tired they were. After the war, they each gave two written accounts of their escape that are generally similar and agree on the important points. But the four accounts of that night are confused, contradictory, and at best vague. Willis said simply, "I remember incidents, but not the count of days."[16]

Their fatigue also caused a drop in morale, especially after they discovered they were walking in the wrong direction. As they retraced their steps, they became increasingly worried that they had missed the Rhine entirely and were hopelessly lost. Willis recalled that night many years later: "We went carefully along the road leading to the valley, letting ourselves down the steep slope by sliding from tree to tree. No train passed, there was no movement. Had we made a mistake? The Rhine Valley should be more animated. We were in despair, for it seemed as though our night had been for nothing."[17]

The train Willis referred to was the railroad that ran along the Rhine. They expected to hear a train before they saw it, and the sound would help guide them toward the river. What they had forgotten, or did not know, was that trains did not run at night.

Their luck changed as dawn approached. Isaacs told a postwar interviewer: "At about daybreak, just as we were looking for a place to hide, we heard a locomotive's whistle. We decided to keep going until we were in a position to observe the track and the river, and, if possible, the lines of sentries patrolling both. In this way we hoped to discover the number of sentries, their positions and beats, and the hours the watch was changed."[18]

They left the road they were on and made their way through the forest in the direction from which the sound had come. As they approached the river, they were enveloped in a thick fog that reduced visibility to nearly zero. Forward progress became almost impossible, and they decided to climb the next hill. That would at least get them up high enough to see the river. Reaching the top of the hill they "took up a position in the bush and awaited developments."[19]

The fog burned off by 0900 and they saw that they were just a mile from the Rhine. To their left was Hauenstein and behind it lay Waldshut. On the road below they saw a group of German soldiers pushing a milk cart. An hour later they saw smoke rising from from a passing locomotive. When they also saw smoke rising across the river, they were able to confirm the presence of the railroad on the Swiss side.

Throughout the day German civilians passed within a few feet of where they were hiding. Twice civilians discovered them but no one seemed to take any interest. As the day wore on, the pair became bolder. That afternoon they broke cover and moved up to a place where they could get a better view of the river and railroad. Passing civilians continued to be a threat: "All day long pedestrians passed our clump of bushes within two feet of us. We sat behind some brush and peered through trying to see the sentries, but we were unsuccessful owing to the nature of the terrain. We laid our plans for that evening from what little information we did obtain, and then went to sleep."[20]

They awoke at 1900, stripped off their clothes, and greased their bodies with lard to protect themselves from the cold water. They donned their swimsuits, which were nothing more than Red Cross boxer shorts and undershirts, and then put on their outer garments. They rubbed dirt onto their faces and hands, discarded their shoes, raincoat, and knapsacks, and started toward the river.

The fog had returned and, combined with the dark night, made it difficult for them to maintain their bearings. But it also cloaked them and greatly reduced their chances of being seen. They moved slowly and stopped frequently to listen for guards tramping their posts. Hearing none, they crossed two small roads and a railroad branch line without seeing any sign of a sentry. They reached the railroad tracks along the river at about 2100 and crossed over them.

As they lay there beside the embankment, they heard the unmistakable sounds of a guard coming toward them along the tracks. They lay motionless, their faces pressed into the earth as the guard passed above them. They waited for the sounds of his boots on the ties to fade before crawling to the edge of a retaining wall along the riverbank. There they found a new, unexpected problem. The wall, Isaacs called it a cliff, was vertical and dropped sixty feet to a gravel road at its base. To make matters worse, the road was guarded and there was a sentry directly below them. Unable to get down the wall, they spent the next three hours searching for a way down to the river.

At about midnight they came to a small stream that flowed toward the river. As they crawled through a patch of dead blackberry bushes along the bank, Willis snapped a dry twig. The crack sounded like an explosion to the two tense men and startled a guard standing nearby. The guard shone the powerful beam of his lantern across the stream but all he could see in the fog was a white haze in front of him. He continued to play the beam around in the direction from which the sound had come for several minutes but remained rooted to his post. Had he walked twenty feet forward, he would have stepped on both men. Finally the light went out.

The two Americans let out a sigh and began moving slowly and cautiously to their left, putting distance between themselves and the German. It had been a very close shave, but at least they knew where the guard was. As soon as they dared, they slid down the stream bank on their bellies and eased into the frigid water. "Our hands and knees and the soles of our feet were cut by the sharp rocks; and the water felt like ice to our badly nourished bodies," Isaacs recalled. "Besides the physical torture, the mental strain we were under was terrible."[21]

The mental strain became nearly intolerable when, while they were crawling under a small bridge, one of them dislodged a rock that fell into the stream. A guard manning a fixed post heard the loud splash and immediately illuminated the streambed with a powerful spotlight. Again the fog saved them. But the tension did not lessen until they were well beyond the bridge because every time they moved the German switched on the light.

They finally reached the Rhine at 0200. It had taken them two hours to crawl a hundred yards. Both men were exhausted, and both were taken back by the ferocity of the river. Willis seriously doubted that Isaacs could survive the swim.

"Once in the Rhine we had to undress in the midst of the terribly swirling current, and Isaacs said he couldn't swim well," Willis recalled. "I felt sure he would drown, for the currents and the whirlpools were worse than you can imagine."[22]

Neither man had expected anything quite like what they were facing. The Rhine at that point was a wild river with a temperature so low that few people could withstand it more than a few minutes. The whirlpools especially were an unpleasant surprise. They appeared and then abruptly disappeared, making ominous sucking and gurgling sounds. The two escapees were standing knee deep in the river, shedding their outer garments, when Willis was knocked off his feet and swept away. It happened so fast that Isaacs did not know his companion was gone until he asked a question and got no answer. Moments later, Isaacs was also caught by the current and swept downriver.

Willis was still wearing his wool trousers when he was swept away.

It was a nightmare. Although I swam with all my strength, the current continually swept me back toward the German shore. Realizing I could make no progress with my trousers on, I managed to undo my belt buckle and slip one leg out with the aid of the other, kicking down with the free foot. I nearly sank. My trousers clung to my feet. I felt myself drowning. Of a sudden I managed to rid myself of my trousers that dragged me down, clutching me like dead hands, and my movements were free again.[23]

Isaacs allowed the current to sweep him downriver while he struggled to get across. The extreme cold was getting to him and he was starting to have cramps. Certain that he was going to drown, he was on the verge of giving up when his body washed onto a sandy spit. From there he tried every stroke he knew to overcome the force of the current, but he was not a strong swimmer and he was already weakened by six days on the run. Virtually helpless, suffering from the early symptoms of hypothermia, he was losing his battle with the river. He did not panic but he knew that he was near death. That knowledge, plus his strong will and determination, caused him to make one last effort. Finally, summoning what was left of his strength, he flailed and kicked without success in a final effort to reach the bank. Spent, he rolled over on his back, closed his eyes, and "commended his soul to his God." At that moment his feet touched bottom and his body came to a halt against the riverbank. Too tired to get up, Isaacs lay there "trying to find words for a proper thanksgiving."[24]

After catching his breath, he walked along the railroad tracks on the Swiss side of the river until he came to a customs post. The border guard, Paul Schäpfer, took Isaacs in, fed him, called the military authorities, and went in search of Willis. He found him in a tavern two miles away.

Puryear

The guards were still shooting when the camp commandant, Oberst Otto Ehrt, and his officers moved to determine how many had gotten out and who they were. It was not an easy task. According to Dr. Gallagher:

> The lights were still out and the guards' lanterns provided inadequate light. Nobody knew how many men had escaped, and the prisoners were milling around and deliberately dragging their heels about forming up to be counted. The Germans would not get an accurate head count until after sun up, and the lights remained out all night.[1]

After taking the roll call, which was part of their standard plan for dealing with escapes, the Germans knew that five men had gotten out of the compound. Whenever prisoners escaped from a camp, guards would immediately start a thorough search of the area around the camp, usually out to a distance of two or three miles. Depending on when the escape took place, that search might last ten or twelve hours. The search at Villingen lasted until about noon the following day. In the meantime, motorcycle couriers and bicycle riders were sent to all the railroad stations within three miles and the local police were notified in the same way. The railroad authorities passed the alarm down the line, and the local police spread the word among their agencies. The nearest military district headquarters then assumed responsibility for the expanded search.

Oberst Ehrt reported the escape to the XIV Military District headquarters in Freiburg, and officers there spread the alarm by telegraph and telephone throughout the entire district, with special alerts to the troops stationed along the Swiss border. Then they sat back and waited. The German policy for dealing with escapes was largely passive but very efficient.[2]

George Puryear planned to meet Caxton Tichener about a quarter of a mile from the camp. There was no specific spot, just a general location that both thought would be easy to find. All along, they had been working on the assumption that since they were going out the same window together, they would be able to stay together—or at least remain within sight of one another. That assumption proved to be false.

Once he was safely in the forest, Puryear "went to the prearranged spot where we were to meet and waited fifteen minutes. While I waited there were about fifty shots fired. No one came, so I got down on my knees, prayed for luck and started off."[3] He had correctly concluded that Tichener had either been captured or killed, or had taken a widely divergent route away from the camp. In either case, there would be no rendezvous.

Alone, Puryear was only slightly better prepared than he had been for his escape attempt at Rastatt. The Russian overcoat he had on was made of heavy wool, which would keep him warm but do nothing to keep out the rain that had begun falling heavily. On the plus side, he had acquired a good pair of British boots with hobnailed soles, and he had an extra pair of socks. However, he was short of rations. His food supply consisted of Red Cross biscuits, some sugar cubes, and a can of already-opened hash. The biscuits were in no danger of spoiling, but the hash would have to be eaten soon. His survival equipment included six matches wrapped in oilcloth and a heavy Case pocketknife with two blades. He also had a fairly large homemade compass that was both robust and accurate, and a reasonably accurate hand-drawn map of the Black Forest region south of Villingen and west to Freiburg.

By 0200 on the seventh, Puryear, who had been free for less than four hours, was already showing signs of the brash overconfidence that was the hallmark of his personality. Despite advice to the contrary, he began walking boldly along a road as soon as he got away from the camp. Looking back, it is possible that his behavior, rather than being brash, was indicative of a foxlike cleverness. While the others were heading toward Switzerland in a generally southerly direction, Puryear was headed due west. Going that way made no sense since it was taking him away from

Figure 20. A hand-made compass hidden in a shaving cream container. It was used by George Puryear during his march to Switzerland. Author's collection

Switzerland and would only cost him time. In fact, Puryear reasoned that he would lose the first day entirely. Yet he was willing to make that sacrifice because he figured that the Germans, expecting the fugitives to take the most direct route to Switzerland, would not be looking for a prisoner traveling westward from the camp.[4] In effect he was putting distance between himself and the camp while at the same time letting the search go past him. He could make up the lost day when he turned south.

His logic was sound. The Germans were concentrating their search in a triangular area with a baseline that crossed the Schaffhausen salient from Waldshut to Büsslingen and had Villingen its apex. The area in which Puryear was walking lay outside the triangle. But he was also traveling in an area in which there were two large POW camps—Villingen and Vörenbach, the latter of which was just five miles down the road on which he was walking.

Even if the alarm had not been raised in the area through which Puryear was moving, the local populace was still very suspicious of strangers. Thus, walking on the road, even in the early morning hours, was risky because of the possibility of encountering a German civilian. Despite the risk he was taking, Puryear must be given credit for the way he dealt with the problem. The terrain that lay ahead was even more rugged than that which Tucker and Battle faced. The section of the Black Forest through which Puryear was traveling had peaks ranging from twenty-four hundred to thirty-nine hundred feet in elevation. It was raining steadily, the temperature at night dropped to near freezing, and there was little hope of finding shelter along the way. Puryear's goal was Waldshut, approximately thirty-two miles southwest of Villingen. Knowing that, and knowing that he was poorly equipped for the walk, it was obvious to Puryear that he had to reach Switzerland before his strength gave out from exhaustion, hunger, and exposure. Time was critical, and he knew the quickest way to reach Switzerland in the shortest time was to walk along the roads. It was a gamble, and Puryear was a gambler.

When dawn broke on the seventh, Puryear was about nine miles west and "a little south" of the prison camp. He had made almost no progress toward the Swiss border. He had also continued walking after daybreak. He was nearing the village of Fuchsloch, easily identified by its church spire, when he started to hunt for a place to hole up for the day. It had been a busy day and a hectic night, and he needed rest. It was fully light when he saw two woodcutters coming along the road toward him. When they were still fifty yards away he stepped off the road and disappeared into the bushes, watching silently as the two men passed his hiding place. As soon as he thought they were far enough down the road, he stepped back onto the trail. He watched the woodcutters, whose backs were to him, for a moment. Then, satisfied that he had not been noticed, he turned and nearly collided with a German civilian standing less than ten feet away. The man was clearly watching him, probably attracted by the American's suspicious behavior and odd dress. For a brief moment they looked directly at each other. Puryear had the good sense not to stop and stare or show surprise. Recovering quickly, he "feigned indifference to him, adjusted my clothes leisurely, and strode away as if he meant nothing to me. Thanks to my Russian costume, he was not suspicious and did not follow."[5]

Puryear was right about the fellow not following him, but there is little doubt that he was suspicious. Because of his close encounter with the civilian, Puryear chose to continue on for another mile before going to ground. If the man did summon the police, it would do little good to hide in the immediate area. After a short search, Puryear found a good hiding place and settled in for the day. He changed his socks and ate all his hash "because being open it wouldn't keep."[6]

He also spent some time studying his map and planning the next night's march. His immediate goal was Neustadt, which was about seven or eight miles away. He judged that he could reach Neustadt by the following morning. However, that would leave him in an exposed position close to a population center at dawn. He decided instead to make for the village of Schattenhof that night and wait until the third night to pass through Neustadt. Satisfied with his plan, he bedded down and spent the remainder of the day sleeping fitfully.

7–8 OCTOBER 1918

The careful search the Germans conducted on the seventh was a bit like closing the barn door after the horse has gone. They marched the Russians out of the camp just after dawn and ordered the Americans to fall in on the tennis courts at the compound's west end. While the Americans stood in ranks, the Germans literally tore apart the barracks—both Russian and American. Their efforts were well rewarded. Hiding places inside the walls, under the floors, and in the rafters overhead yielded a treasure trove of compasses, maps, civilian clothes, and implements of all sorts. They also found hidden food but did not seize it because food was not considered contraband.[7]

Oberst Ehrt waited until the guards concluded their search and then personally read a new set of camp rules to the prisoners. No prisoner would be allowed in the compound after dark. All prisoners would be in their beds by 2200. There would be no more parole walks, no piano playing, and no singing. Satisfied that he had squelched any future escape attempts, Oberst Ehrt dismissed them. As the colonel and his executive officer walked toward the main gate, five prisoners led by Norman Archibald of the 95th Aero Squadron, sauntered over to the bathhouse. They were digging a tunnel.[8]

Meanwhile, Puryear spent an uneventful day hidden in a small, shrub-covered depression about thirty yards off the road while the Germans tore the camp apart. The skies remained clear that day and he stripped off his wet clothes and hung them on the bushes around him. But despite the fine weather and the almost total silence of the forest, he slept fitfully. During the times he was awake he rearranged his clothing and donned those pieces that were already dry. By sundown he was again fully dressed and reasonably warm.

In keeping with his generally nonconformist attitude, Puryear broke cover before dark on the evening of the seventh. However, instead of returning to the road, he struck out cross-country. For a man who had already lost a day traveling west, and for whom time was critical, it was an odd decision. But his encounter with the woodcutters and the civilian that morning had rattled him. He was also fooled by the surrounding countryside. What little he could see appeared to be reasonably easy to cross. There were no high peaks to climb, and there did not seem to be any deep ravines or valleys. In fact, the highest point he could see was the Steinberg, about three miles away and only some two hundred feet higher than where he was standing.

He optimistically headed south, making good time until he came to marshy ground as he approached a stream known as the Loch. At first the ground was spongy with only an occasional puddle. However, as he continued on the water rose and the ground fell off sharply. Suddenly he found himself in water up to his waist. Not realizing how large the marsh was, he chose to go on rather than return to dry ground and set a new course. Going back meant losing time. After another hour of splashing through the swamp and making little headway he finally gave up and returned to the road.

His adventure in the marsh cost him two or three hours and left him soaked to the skin. All but one package of his Red Cross biscuits were ruined. As much to keep warm as to make up the time lost, Puryear alternated walking and jogging as he hurried down the road. Besides violating the unwritten rule of avoiding roads, Puryear was about to break several more rules, including entering a populated area to find food. About midnight he raided his first garden. As he approached the first signs of habitation on the outskirts of a small village named Schollach, he spotted a house at the edge of the road. The house was dark, there appeared to be no one about, and there was a small garden on the side of the house. He entered the garden through a gate and quickly gathered up potatoes and turnips, taking only what he could easily carry. It would not be the last time he took such a risk. After eating some of the vegetables he pocketed the rest, planning to eat them during the day, "when it would be impossible to search for anything. I lived more upon these raw foods than upon my scanty rations. Each morning, a little before time to hide, I would collect my day's supply."[9]

It started to rain while Puryear was in the garden stealing potatoes and turnips. He did not mind at first because he was soaked to the skin. His Russian overcoat felt like it weighed a ton and water sloshed in his shoes. He was cold, dead tired, and his wet feet hurt. At about 0400 he started to look for a place to hide and came upon "the only barn I ever saw in Germany that was not either partially inhabited by the people themselves, or so near their houses as to be useless as a hiding place. It stood in a pasture by itself and looked inviting."[10]

He approached the structure cautiously until he was certain there were no people in it. He was doubly surprised—and very pleased—when he discovered that there were no animals inside. Disturbed farm animals had been the undoing of many escapees. Finding the barn was a stroke of good luck, but finding one that was completely empty was even better. The door was not locked and the wet hinges did not groan or squeak when he eased it open and slipped inside. The floor was empty but farm equipment hung from or was stacked against the walls. Obviously the barn was not abandoned. Puryear climbed into the loft fully expecting to find hay in which to bury himself. Much to his disappointment there was none. Still, it was a roof over his head. He stretched out on the wooden floor of the loft in his wet clothes and fell asleep almost immediately.

Puryear covered only about seven miles on the night of 7–8 October. His relatively slow progress was due in part to the time he lost in the marsh and because he stopped three hours early when he found the barn. By comparison, Isaacs and Willis, who were moving cross-country, were four miles ahead of him on the morning of the eighth. But Puryear's decision to stop early had a practical basis. He planned to pass through Neustadt, the largest town in the southern Black Forest, the next night. He hoped to reach it late in the evening in order to avoid running into citizens on the streets. Whether it was overconfidence or naïveté that governed his reasoning, the idea that he could walk boldly through a major town was characteristic of him. Someone once said that God watches over fools and Englishmen. He should have included Puryear among those who enjoyed divine protection.

8–9 OCTOBER 1918

Puryear slept only a few hours before he was awakened by the cold. Unable to go back to sleep, he spent much of the day doing exercises to keep warm. His clothes dried in the process but his boots remained wet. Between exercise sessions he peered through the cracks in the wall to see what was happening outside. The rain continued until 1600, when Puryear finally decided it was dark enough to push on. As he pulled on his boots in preparation for leaving, the barn door swung open and three men and a boy stepped inside. Puryear froze, hardly daring to breathe. All the warnings about not hiding in barns came back to him. He was sure their arrival spelled his undoing. While the boy played in the dirt, the three men shed their raincoats and set a lantern on a box standing beside the wall. They repaired some of the tools, shared a bottle of home brew, and talked. They stayed in the barn for nearly two hours. "For a while I thought it was all up with me, but they never came into the loft where I was hiding." Sometime after 1800 the men and the boy left and Puryear waited twenty more minutes to be sure they were gone before climbing down the ladder. As he reached out to push the door open he had a disconcerting thought: Suppose they had locked the door?[11]

Despite his late departure, Puryear reached Neustadt at about 2230 on the eighth. It was the biggest risk he had yet taken—and the risk was substantial. He later recalled that "All the roads led through the town. I therefore decided to trust to the similarity of my costume to the German uniform and bluff my way through. Though the streets were mostly deserted, it was not late enough for a wayfarer to be looked upon with particular suspicion. I buttoned my Russian military coat, which was far from shoddy, and set my military cap in a very severe position on the forward part of my head. Assuming a very dignified and forbidding manner, I walked through the town, a rival of the most military Prussian officer ever met."[12]

In 1918, Neustadt was one of the few Black Forest towns with electric lighting. Most of the smaller towns still had gas lamps or no streetlights at all. But the narrow streets were far from well lighted; there were many dark spots and shadows that made visibility poor. The first test came when he approached a group of German soldiers standing in the street outside a Lokal. As Puryear drew nearer to them, one of the soldiers shouted, "Achtung!" and the group snapped to attention and saluted him as he passed. Puryear returned the salute. Not much later he encountered a woman who spoke to him as she passed. Not understanding a word of what she said, he pretended to ignore her with "a bearing so haughty as to not encourage familiarity."[13]

His most frightening experience occurred when he passed a hotel being used to quarter troops. He had hardly cleared the entrance when a German officer stepped out the front door into the street and started to follow him. When Puryear quickened his step, the German did the same. "I have never seen a German walk so fast as he did," he wrote later. "I almost had to drop my dignity in order to prevent him shortening the distance between us. I tried to make speed and hold an external appearance of indifference while internally all was in a turmoil."[14] The "chase" lasted until the two men reached the far side of the town, with Puryear just barely able to maintain his lead. Finally, much to his relief, the German turned right onto a narrow street and disappeared. Puryear continued on at the same pace until he was outside of town.

Just outside Neustadt the road forked. The left fork led to Bonndorf, an easy eight-mile walk that was mostly downhill. That route would have taken him nearly halfway to the Rhine. It also would have put him squarely in the middle of the area affected by the special alert. In any event, it did not matter because he did not know the left fork went to Bonndorf. Instead, Puryear chose the right fork. He believed it was the most direct route to take despite the fact that the road rose steeply up the slope of a thirty-nine-hundred-foot mountain called Hochfirst. The initial climb was not difficult because the road was built for travelers who made the ascent on foot. Puryear was nearly halfway up when it started to rain at about midnight. There were roadside rest areas along the way, usually benches that afforded the traveler a place to sit and enjoy the view. Puryear took the opportunity to sit at one of these and eat a raw turnip, but the dark, rain, and cold prevented him from enjoying the view.

Rested, Puryear started off again. However, he lost the main road in the darkness and wandered off onto a lesser trail that soon vanished entirely. Unable to force himself to retrace his steps, Puryear took out his compass and then struck out "through the forest in a constant rain hoping to soon hit another road leading down on the other side."[15] He was now hopelessly lost. Stumbling forward he fell over a small cliff, rolled down the mountainside, and came to rest on "a ledge covered with low underbrush." He was lucky to get away with just cuts and bruises. The fall had a sobering effect on him. Rather than crashing blindly on down the mountainside, he decided to go up. He hoped to gain the summit, get his bearings, and find a safe route down.

Puryear reached the top of the mountain at about 0230. It was snowing lightly but he was able to see over the tops of the trees and down into the valley. He quickly laid out a course that he hoped would take him to a road. However, the route down proved more difficult than he had expected: "I stepped back into the uncut forest, where because of the underbrush I could hardly make my way. I would stumble and fall, often lying where I fell, almost dropping off to sleep. Always I would wake with a start. Finally I just stumbled onto another road which took me down the mountain. This road conducted me to a proper highway and with the strength I had left, I struck out to make as much progress as possible for the rest of the night."[16]

He made up for lost time by keeping to the road until long after daylight. He passed along the east side of the Titisee and by midmorning was nearing Neuglashütten, which put him almost six miles west of the line he had intended to follow. It was nearly noon before he found a hiding place among some trees a hundred yards off the road. Exhausted, he made a firm decision "to stick to big highways," preferably ones that had a telephone line along them.[17]

Despite his blundering path across the Hochfirst, Puryear had made excellent progress. He was camped within a night's walk of the Rhine, and the fact that he was there at all was proof that luck played a major role in any escapee's success. By all rights, he should have been caught long before he curled up in his hiding place on the morning of the ninth.

9–10 OCTOBER 1918

Puryear made rapid progress when he set out shortly after dark on the ninth. The road he was on led him along the south shore of the Schluchtsee, avoiding the four-thousand-foot-high peaks to his right. Although the relatively level road went through or near the villages of

Unterkummern, Eisenbreche, and Muchenland, the few people he encountered along the way ignored him and he ignored them. A short distance north of Häusern, his track crossed the trail Isaacs and Willis would take several hours later. Had he been moving more slowly or had he started later, he might have run into them.

He entered Häusern at 2300 and passed through the town without incident. When he emerged, he found a road sign pointing toward Waldshut and the Rhine. At last certain of his position and the direction he needed to go, Puryear set off for Waldshut. It was just a little after midnight on the tenth and he had at least another five hours of darkness. Shortly before dawn he reached the outskirts of Schmitzeningen and stopped. He was just over a mile from the Rhine, and he could smell it.

Throughout his journey Puryear had traveled almost exclusively along roads and made no serious effort to avoid towns and villages. He had slept in a barn, stolen vegetables from beneath a window, and exchanged greetings with other travelers. He had violated all of conventional wisdom's hard and fast rules. Although his actions were dangerous, naive, and maybe even stupid, they had gotten him almost to his goal.

The extreme cold on the tenth kept him awake most of the day. Yet despite his fatigue and discomfort, his spirits were high because he knew that when nightfall came he would "come to the passage of the last ditch—the Rhine—that night."[18] That is, if nothing went wrong. As soon as it was dark, Puryear "took off all my clothes and put on first those in which I intended to make the swim, adjusting them very snugly and tightly, taking up all the slack in the strings. Over these I put my other clothing to keep me warm until the time came."[19]

His swimsuit, intended to help retain body heat in the frigid water, was actually a set of cotton long johns to which he had attached strings at the wrists, ankles, and waist. Puryear was drawing on his boyhood experience gained from swimming in the Cumberland River near his home in Gallatin, Tennessee. His initial preparations complete, he made himself as comfortable as possible, and waited for nightfall.

Puryear ate all the food he had left before setting out on the night of 10–11 October. In his mind, he was embarking on a do-or-die mission and he needed all the energy he could muster. Continuing to use the main road, he reached the outer limits of Landshut at 2300 and immediately turned right to circle the town. An hour later he was lying flat atop a hill, his map before him, studying the river to be sure the other side was really Switzer-land. "Some of the boys would use different means of designating Swit-zerland," he wrote after the war. "I had labeled the Swiss territory on my map, 'the promised Land.' And I wondered, while standing on this moun-tain looking over into Switzerland, if I, like Moses, would only be allowed thus to look into it. Having satisfied myself that the country which I saw before me was Switzerland, I began to plan my swim."[20]

The landmarks that convinced him he was in the right place were a railroad line and a major vehicle road that ran parallel to the river on the German side. Puryear said later that he had a clear view of the river even though the night was very dark. The spot he picked for the crossing was a place where he believed the shape of the bend would cause the current to push him toward the Swiss side. He also noted a reverse bend about a mile farther downriver that would have the opposite effect. He had to complete his crossing before being swept around the second bend because the cur-rent below it would deposit him back on German soil.

He studied the river for nearly three hours, searching for sentries and watching for patrols. He once saw a searchlight beam sweep the river sur-face and then go out. The light came from somewhere upriver. As he lay there watching and listening he heard sounds that gave him cause for concern: "The swift current kept up a ceaseless roar, punctuated by the noise of whirlpools which came and went here and yonder. It was not a comfortable sound. When one of them would form, as it reached its cli-max, the surrounding water filled up the hole made in the center by the whirlpool, and sent up a loud gurgling sound."[21]

He also gave thought to the river's frigid temperature, which, combined with the fast-running current and numerous whirlpools, led the Germans to believe the Rhine was impassable. He "knew the temperature was so low that no ordinary constitution was strong enough to withstand it more than a few minutes, and I recalled a story about a cemetery in Basel that was filled with Russians who had tried to make the swim. But I had known and considered these things from the beginning, and they didn't disturb me now."[22]

By 0400 on the eleventh he was satisfied that the place where he planned to cross was clear. He stripped off all his outer garments except his olive drab shirt, which he kept on "to cover the whiteness of my undershirt," and started down the slope toward the river.[23] He held his open Case knife in his right hand. He later said that he had not brought the knife along with the intent of "using it as a means of violence," since that "would get one in great difficulty if captured afterwards." But as he crept toward the river in the hours before dawn, he vowed that "if anyone attempted to stop me just on the border, I would stop at nothing rather than be taken."[24]

He reached the railroad embankment, crawled to the top, and looked in both directions. There was no sign of movement in either direction. Ahead of him, just a few yards away, he could hear the river's "ceaseless roar, punctuated by the noise of whirlpools."[25] As soon as he was satisfied that the way was clear, he rose and darted across the tracks, then dropped flat on the ground at the edge of the road. Again he looked carefully in both directions. The road was made of flat, hard-packed gravel and was about thirty feet wide. Just across the road the ground dropped off sharply to the water's edge. After looking one more time to be sure the way was clear, he rose to a crouching position and, moving in a low crouch, ran across the road. He dropped down into the heavy bushes and grass growing along the riverbank and listened. There were no sounds of pursuit, just the roar of the river and the gurgling of the whirlpools. From the direction of Waldshut he heard a church bell strike five, and "knew the exact time of crossing the river."[26] He also knew that dawn was fast approaching.

Puryear shed his outer clothes, hung his shoes around his neck, and waded into the water. He had expected it to be cold, but the shock when he entered the river nearly took away his breath. The current was also much stronger than he had expected—a fact he realized when it knocked him off his feet. Caught in the current's strong grip, he found that his shoes were a hindrance and let them go. His estimate that the current would carry him toward the Swiss side proved correct until he reached mid-stream. There he discovered that it had "a tendency to hold me there, and I knew then that the time for my utmost effort was at hand."[27]

The water's nearly freezing temperature was already starting to affect him. He became dizzy, had difficulty breathing, and felt as though he was "losing his grip on himself."[28] In a state of near panic, he started swimming hard for the far bank. The surge of adrenaline that accompanied the effort helped clear his head. As he drew slowly closer to the Swiss side he was still being swept downriver like "an express train." At that rate he would soon enter the second bend, which would push him back toward Germany. Moreover, the cold was taking a "firmer hold." He began to panic and, in his confused state, he also started to worry that he would "at any moment strike a whirlpool." Certain that he was nearing the second bend, Puryear made a last desperate effort to reach the Swiss shore. It paid off—his hand struck the river bottom.[29] As soon as he felt it, he tried to stand up. However, the current bowled him over. Coughing and sputtering, he flailed his arms and feet, trying to grip the bottom.

"With every step I went downstream fifteen or twenty feet," he recalled. "After a few steps, and when very close, the bottom disappeared and I had to swim again. I was in the second bend, and the bank being steep and well washed was passing me like an express train. At first my grasp at the bank was futile. But I snatched and clawed along for a good many feet and finally succeeded in stopping."[30]

It was nearly dawn when Puryear dragged himself out of the Rhine and lay exhausted on the Swiss side of the river. He had been a prisoner for seventy-eight days and he had escaped. He did not know it then, but he was the first American officer to escape from the Germans and return to Allied control.[31]

Puryear quickly located a Swiss railroad worker who took him in, gave him warm clothes and something to eat, and escorted him to a Swiss army post. Puryear said it "was a rather long walk."[32] The railroad employee turned him over to an English-speaking soldier who gave him a Swiss army uniform to wear. Later that day the Swiss put him on a train to Zurich, where he was given a complete physical by the Swiss authorities. He spent the night in Reinfelden.

The following morning, the twelfth, he had a rather amusing experience when the Swiss tried to turn him over to the Americans in Bern. Accompanied by a Swiss army captain, Puryear was to be met in Bern by a Captain Davis, the American military attaché. When he stepped off the train in Bern with the Swiss officer, Puryear was still wearing a Swiss uniform. Davis, on the other hand, was wearing civilian clothes. Davis was looking for a Swiss officer with an American in civilian clothes and Puryear was looking for someone in an American uniform. The result was that both men walked right past each other.[33]

Unable to deliver his ward, the Swiss captain took Puryear to the Swiss army headquarters in Bern. Davis showed up four hours later and collected Puryear from the Swiss. The first thing he did was take Puryear to a clothier and buy him a complete set of civilian clothes.

Epilogue

The Swiss turned Isaacs and Willis over to the American embassy in Bern on 15 October. There they were given civilian clothes, passports, and cash. They, along with Puryear, posed for photographers, filled out Red Cross questionnaires, and provided information to the American military attaché about conditions in Germany. On the eighteenth the embassy staff sent the three men to Paris by train. There they were split up.

The French released Willis from service and sent him home. Isaacs went to London and reported to Rear Adm. William S. Sims. Ironically, the military intelligence information he had worked so desperately to deliver was outdated. Puryear went to the AEF Air Service headquarters at Tours where he was received as a hero. He met Gen. John J. Pershing, the AEF commander, had lunch with Billy Mitchell, and appeared in two early newsreel clips that were shown nationwide in 1918. General Mitchell then sent him on a speaking tour to all U.S. Air Service squadrons in France. His topic was what to expect as a POW and how to escape. His tour had hardly started when the war ended and General Mitchell recalled him to Tours and told him he was going home.[1]

Everybody was eager to go home after the armistice was signed, none more so than the POWs. Some of them disappeared quickly and left no mark beyond the entries in their wartime records. A few achieved post-war prominence. What follows are the added details I was able to find about some of the men who took part in the mass escape from Villingen.

The Germans returned Blanchard Battle to Villingen on 14 October and locked him in solitary confinement for eighteen days. While he was there, the Germans charged him with mutiny, found him guilty, and sentenced him to serve out the rest of the war in a reprisal camp near Berlin. On 3 November he and two guards started out by train for Berlin, but they never got there. By the time they reached Kassel on the eighth, Germany was in revolt. Revolutionaries from a naval infantry battalion boarded the train, disarmed the guards, and freed Battle.[2]

Taking advantage of the opportunity, he convinced one of the sailors to accompany him to Holland, and the two set out in that direction. They reached the Dutch border the day after the armistice was signed, but the civilian commander of a group of revolutionary guards turned them back. The civilian told Battle to return to Villingen and ordered the sailor to remain with him. Battle obtained money from the civilian and boarded a train headed south. However, instead of going to Villingen, Battle got off in Frankfurt and took a room in a hotel. That evening he struck up a conversation with a German officer in the hotel bar. The officer had joined the revolutionaries and when Battle broached the subject of going to Holland the officer advised him to return to Villingen and await repatriation there. To enforce his suggestion, he placed Battle under guard for the rest of the night.

The following morning, accompanied by his guard, Battle boarded another train headed toward Villingen. Along the way he tried to bribe the guard to help him get to Holland. The guard, "who still possessed a strong respect for authority, wired ahead for reinforcements." Thwarted in his attempts to get home early, Battle resigned himself to waiting in Villingen for repatriation. On 26 November, he and nearly two hundred other Americans at Villingen were taken by train to Konstanz and then into Switzerland. The war was over and Battle was finally a free man.[3]

General Mitchell never forgot or forgave Maj. Harry Brown, who he accused of losing an entire squadron intact to the Germans. No charges were ever filed against Brown and the degree of his responsibility for the unhappy affair is debatable. Nevertheless, the events of 10 July ruined his army career and he resigned his commission in 1920. He died on 2 March 1960 at the age of sixty-nine.[4]

The Germans court-martialed Rowan Tucker, found him guilty, and sentenced him to confinement in the prison fortress at Ingolstadt, also known as Fort 9. The Germans were still processing Tucker's paperwork when the war abruptly ended. He returned to the camp's general population and was released with the others on 29 November.

Edouard Isaacs went home to a hero's welcome that got him embroiled in a public fight between Rear Admiral Sims and Secretary of the Navy Josephus Daniels. At issue was the award of Isaacs's Medal of Honor, which Admiral Sims did not believe Isaacs deserved. The admiral's caustic comment that "he didn't do anything but get himself captured by the enemy" was widely printed in the nation's newspapers and made the war between the admiral and Daniels even more bitter. The observation was not entirely accurate, and Isaacs's Medal of Honor was just the tip of the iceberg. Daniels also planned to award Navy Crosses and a host of lesser awards to officers who had never been in combat, many of whom spent the entire war at a desk in Washington, D.C. Sims objected to what he considered to be cheapening the awards. In Isaacs's case, the admiral felt that the lieutenant had simply done what was expected of him. He agreed that Isaacs was entitled to an award, but the Medal of Honor was over doing it. Daniels and his assistant, Franklin D. Roosevelt, strongly supported awarding the Medal of Honor to Isaacs because of the injuries he suffered on 6 July at the hands of the two guards on the train from which he tried to escape. The fight was public and it was ugly, but Daniels won.

Isaacs, who never fully recovered from those injuries, retired from the navy in 1921. He changed his name to Izac in 1925 and worked for the *San Diego Union* until 1927. In the years immediately following the war, he developed a lasting friendship with Franklin Roosevelt and capitalized on that relationship in 1936, winning San Diego's congressional seat. He remained in Congress until he was voted out in 1948. Izac died on 18 January 1990 at the age of one hundred.[5]

Harold Willis returned to the Boston architectural firm of Allen and Collins as a partner. The firm became Allen, Collins, and Willis, and he became one of America's leading ecclesiastical architects. His church designs are still considered among the most beautiful in the country. During World War II Willis designed air bases for the Army Air Forces (AAF) Ferry Command and later became the chief tactical liaison officer for the AAF in North Africa. He died on 17 April 1962 at the age of seventy-three.[6]

Although the only medal George Puryear received was the World War I Victory Medal with clasp, he still received a hero's welcome back home.

One of America's most popular weekly magazines, the *Atlantic Monthly*, published his first-person account of his POW experiences.

Unlike most of his friends, Puryear stayed in the Air Service after the war and served with the 9th Aero Squadron at Rockwell Field in San Diego. On 20 October 1919 he flew from Rockwell to a border field at Calexico, California, where he was to drop off the payroll and have lunch. He expected to be back at Rockwell not later than 1700 that day.[7]

Because of carburetor problems with his DeHavilland DH-4, he took off from San Diego two hours late. He arrived at Calexico shortly before noon after an uneventful flight, delivered the payroll, and went to the officers' mess to have lunch. While he was there the mechanics refueled his plane and moved it out onto the runway for a 1300 takeoff. But another delay, again caused by carburetor trouble, pushed the takeoff time back to 1430.

When Puryear climbed back into the cockpit that afternoon he had a total of 200 hours flying time, sixteen of which were in the DH-4. He was a competent pilot and what occurred ten minutes later should never have happened. At 1430 he headed the DH-4 down the runway, the tail came up, the wheels left the ground, and Puryear started his climb. It was a beautiful day for flying.[8]

The DH-4 was two hundred feet up when the Liberty engine suddenly stopped running. At that point Puryear was not in serious trouble. There was a cotton field at the end of the runway and all he had to do was drop the nose and glide to a landing. It was a procedure that flight instructors and squadron commanders had hammered into him ever since he was a flying cadet.

Going down in the cotton field posed no exceptional danger. There was a pretty good chance that he might tear off the under carriage, and there was a fair chance that the plane might nose over after it touched down. But those were only possibilities, not probabilities. However, it was dead certain that his plane would stall and crash if he attempted to bank and turn back toward the runway. Unfortunately, that is exactly what he did. Witnesses on the ground saw the powerless aircraft bank to the right, lose lift, and fall. The right wing hit the ground and the plane cartwheeled across the desert, killing Puryear almost instantly.[9]

Notes

INTRODUCTION

1. I have based my discussion here on a broad study of WWI escapes. There were about 190,000 British POWs, of whom roughly 500 attempted to escape. There were more than 500,000 French POWs, of whom some 1,000 made at least one escape attempt. The figures on American POWs are available in RG120, Microfilm Publication M990, "Gorrell's Histories of the American Expeditionary Forces Air Service, 1917–1919," roll 42, ser. M, vols. 6–11, "Experiences of Air Service Officers Who Were Prisoners of War," Military Reference Branch, National Archives, Washington, D.C. (hereafter cited as NA; documents from this microfilm publication will hereafter be cited as M990 followed by the roll number and file name); RG200, Records of the American National Red Cross, 1917–34, Files Pertaining to the Bureau of Prisoners' Information and Communication, 6 April 1917 to 31 December 1918, "Escaped American Prisoners" file, Civil Reference Branch, NA (hereafter cited as RG200 followed by the file name); and Leonard P. Ayres, *The War With Germany: A Statistical Summary*, "Table 10. Battle Casualties in the American Expeditionary Forces," p. 122.
2. Ibid.

SGT. HAROLD WILLIS, LAFAYETTE ESCADRILLE

1. Dennis Gordon, *Lafayette Escadrille Pilot Biographies*, p. 174.
2. Ibid.
3. Carl P. Dennett, *Prisoners of the Great War*, pp. 110–14.
4. Ibid., pp. 114–17.
5. H. C. Armstrong, ed., *Escape*, p. 294.

LT. EDOUARD ISAACS, USN

1. RG242, Records of the German Navy, 1850–1945, Microfilm Publication T-1022, roll 614, PG61673, "Kriegstagebuch des Unterseebootes U-90," Military Reference Branch, NA.
2. Ibid.
3. Ibid.
4. RG45, Naval Records Collection, 1911–1927, USS *President Lincoln* file, "Report by Commanding Officer," Military Reference Branch, NA (hereafter cited as RG45 followed by the file name).
5. Ibid.
6. RG45, Edouard Isaacs, *Prisoner of the U-90;* and Arnold Fischdick, *U-90: Kameradschaft und Erlebnisse im Ubootkrieg,* pp. 98–99.
7. Actually, Remy had second thoughts and returned to the area an hour later to make another search for the captain ("Kriegstagebuch des Unterseebootes U-90").
8. RG45, Naval Records Collection, 1911–1927, USS *President Lincoln* File, "Testimony of Lt. Edouard V. Isaacs Relating to His Capture and Subsequent Escape Attempts," National Archives (hereafter cited as Isaacs Testimony).
9. Interview with Jerry A. O'Callaghn, Ph.D., Arlington, Va., 1 February 1992. Dr. Callaghn was a close friend of Edouard Isaacs.

1ST LT. BLANCHARD BATTLE, AIR SERVICE, AEF

1. M990, roll 36, ser. J, vol. 9, Third Aviation Instruction Center, Issoudun, "Report of the Headquarters Department."
2. George C. Kenny and Horace M. Guilbert, *History of the 91st Aero Squadron, U.S. Air Service,* p. 3.
3. Norman Franks, et al. *The Jasta Pilots,* pp. 70–71, 80.
4. "Experiences of Air Service Officers": Battle, Blanchard, and Williamson, Joseph.
5. I first heard the expression during WWII from a Corsair pilot whose plane had gone into San Francisco Bay near Alameda Naval Air Station. I heard the expression again from Capt. Tom Pollock, USN (Ret.), who said the expression was common when he was a naval aviation cadet in 1939.
6. "Experiences of Air Service Officers": frames 749–1002.
7. "Experiences of Air Service Officers": Battle and Williamson.
8. Ibid.

1ST LT. HERBERT ALLEN "TOOTS" WARDLE, AIR SERVICE, AEF

1. RG18, Records of the Army Air Force, 1907–1947, box 618, "Memphis Examining Board to CSO," 1 May 1917, Military Reference Branch, NA.
2. Ibid.
3. "Experiences of Air Service Officers": Wardle, Herbert A.
4. Ibid.
5. Ibid.
6. William M. Russell, *The Happy Warrior: Letters of William Muir Russell, an American Aviator in the Great War, 1917–1918*, p. 56.
7. "Experiences of Air Service Officers": Wardle.
8. Ibid.
9. Armstrong, ed., *Escape*, pp. 380–83.
10. "Experiences of Air Service Officers": Wardle.
11. Armstrong, ed., *Escape*, pp. 386–87.
12. "Experiences of Air Service Officers": Wardle.
13. Ibid.

1ST Lt. CARLYLE "DUSTY" RHODES, AIR SERVICE, AEF

1. Harold Buckley, *Squadron 95*, p. 41.
2. Ibid., p. 64.
3. Ibid.
4. M990, roll 19, ser. N, vol. 7, "History of the 95th Aero Squadron."
5. Buckley, *Squadron 95*, p. 83.
6. "Experiences of Air Service Officers": Rhodes, Carlyle.
7. Buckley, *Squadron 95*, p. 83.

1ST LT. WILLIAM CHALMERS, AIR SERVICE, AEF

1. New England Aviators Publishing Committee, *New England Aviators, 1914–1918*, p. 1:92.
2. Buckley, *Squadron 95*, p. 24.
3. M990, roll 19, "History of the 94th Aero Squadron," frames 137–38.
4. "Experiences of Air Service Officers": Chalmers, William W.
5. "History of the 95th Aero Squadron," frame 433; and Buckley, *Squadron 95*, pp. 93–94. According to USAF Historical Study no.133, *U.S. Air Service Victory Credits in World War I*, Sewall did not receive credit for this victory.

MAJ. HARRY BROWN AND THE 96TH AERO SQUADRON

1. M990, roll 19, ser. E, vol. 14, "History of the 96th Aero Squadron."
2. Charles Codman, *Contact: The History of the 96th Aero Squadron in the Great War,* p. 47.
3. "Experiences of Air Service Officers": McChesney, Joseph.
4. Ibid.: Mellen, Joseph, and Tucker, Rowan.
5. Ibid.: Browning, Robert, and Duke, James.
6. Ibid.: Ratterman, George, and Smith, Herbert.
7. Ibid.: Lewis, Henry, and Tichener, Caxton.
8. Ibid.: MacDonald, Durward, and Strong, Alfred.
9. "96th Aero Squadron Daily Log, 12 June–7 December 1918," Thomas G. Miller Collection, U.S. Army Military History Institute, Carlisle Barracks, Pa.
10. Ibid.
11. Brig. Gen. William Mitchell, "Mitchell Diaries," Library of Congress, Washington, D.C., p. 247.

2D LT. GEORGE H. CROWNS, IOTH FIELD ARTILLERY

1. *The German Offensive of 15 July 1918,* pp. 510, 552, 765.
2. Ibid., doc. 642, "Extracts from the Diary of Capt. A. Brigham, Jr., 10th F.A.," pp. 878–79.
3. Ibid., doc. 370, "War Diary German 10th Division," pp. 508–15.
4. "Extracts from the Diary of Capt. A. Brigham," pp. 878–79.

IST LT. GEORGE W. PURYEAR, AIR SERVICE, AEF

1. George Puryear, "The Airman's Escape," *Atlantic Monthly,* January and February 1919, p. 452.
2. Ibid.
3. Ibid.
4. Gustavus A. Puryear, no title, n.d., three-page typescript of William Puryear's Civil War experience, Puryear Family Papers held by William P. Puryear (hereafter cited as Puryear Family Papers).

FRIEDRICHSFESTE, RASTATT

1. "Die Festung Rastatt," Stadt Karlstuhe, Stadtbibliothek, Archiv Sammlungen, pp. 11-13.
2. Bernard James Gallagher, diary entry for 2 May 1918, copy in the possession of William B. Gallagher, M.D. (Hereafter cited as Gallagher Diary.)
3. "Die Festung Rastatt."

4. This account of Chalmers's and Crowns's escape is taken entirely from "Experiences of Air Service Officers": Chalmers, William.
5. Ibid.
6. George W. Puryear papers in the possession of William Puryear (hereafter cited as George Puryear Papers); Puryear, "Airman's Escape," p. 456; "Die Festung Rastatt," pp. 11–15; and "Experiences of Air Service Officers": Puryear, George.
7. Puryear, "Airman's Escape," pp. 455–56.
8. Ibid.
9. Ibid.
10. Ibid.
11. Ibid.
12. Ibid.
13. Ibid.

THE LISTENING HOTEL, KARLSRUHE

1. Codman, *Contact*, p. 166; and Stadt Karlsruhe Stadtarchiv letter to author, 29 September 1993.
2. "Experiences of Air Service Officers": Puryear.
3. The following description of the Listening Hotel and the methods used there are a composite of many sources. The most readily available published sources are Edouard Isaacs, *Prisoner of the U-90* (Boston & New York: Houghton Mifflin Co., 1919) pp. 46–50; Charles Codman, *Contact* (Boston: Little, Brown, and Co., 1937) pp. 166–78; and Norman Archibald, *Heaven High and Hell Deep* (New York: Albert & Charles Boni, Inc., 1935) pp. 247–59. Addiditonal descriptions are found in the individual reports written by former POWs after the war. Those can be found in "Experiences of Air Service Officers": frames 749–1002.
4. RG45, Edouard Isaacs, "Special Report on Experiences as a Prisoner of War in Germany."
5. George Puryear Papers.
6. Gallagher Diary, 20 May 1918.
7. "Experiences of Air Service Officers": Battle.

KARLSRUHE MAIN CAMP

1. Unless otherwise noted, the description of the Karlsruhe main camp that follows is taken from the following sources: "Offizier-Kriegsgefangenenlager und Lagerplan," Generallandesarchiv Karlsruhe, Standort Karlsruhe; William C. Levere, *The History of Sigma Alpha Epsilon in the Great War,* pp. 332–36; RG200, File 140.18, Bureau of Prisoners Relief, 1917–1919, pt. IV, "Camps, S-W Villingen"; and Kurt Kranich, "Karlsruhe: Schicksalstage einer Stadt," Stadt Karlsruhe, Stadtbibliothek, Archiv Sammlungen, 1973.

2. The information on the French air raid on Karlsruhe is found in Kranich, "Karlsruhe: Schicksalstage einer Stadt."

3. Ibid.

4. Puryear, "Airman's Escape," p. 457.

5. Isaacs, "Special Report on Experiences as a Prisoner."

6. Unless otherwise noted, the following account is found in Isaacs, *Prisoner of the U-90*, and Isaacs, "Special Report on Experiences as a Prisoner."

7. Isaacs, *Prisoner of the U-90*, p. 63.

8. Ibid., p. 64.

9. Ibid., p. 65.

10. Ibid., pp. 70–71.

11. Ibid., pp. 85–86.

TRAUSNITZ CASTLE

1. Schloss-pflegerakten Landshut, Rep. 151, VIII Militär und Kriegsspilal, File 101 "Gefangenunterkunft auf der Burg Trausnitz, 1915–1918," Bayerischer Staatsarchiv, Burg Trausnitz, Landshut; and "Landshut/Burg Trausnitz," Bayerische Verwaltung der staatlichen Schlösser, Garten und Seen, pp. 1–55. The description is also based on the author's observations made at the castle in August, 1994.

2. Puryear, " Airman's Escape," p. 458.

3. "Experiences of Air Service Officers": Batty, Brian.

4. Interview with Joseph Prangl, Staatliche Schlossverwaltung, Burg Trausnitz, 24 August 1994; "Gefangenunterkunft auf der Burg Trausnitz, 1915–1918"; and "Landshut/Burg Trausnitz," pp. 1-55.

5. Unless otherwise noted, the following account is derived from "Experiences of Air Service Officers": Hall, Norman; Mellen, Joseph; Strong, Alfred; and Tucker, Rowan; Norman Archibald, *Heaven High, Hell Deep: 1917–1918*, pp. 283–84; and the George Puryear Papers.

6. "Experiences of Air Service Officers": Brown, Harry; and "Camps, S-W Villingen."

7. Unless otherwise noted, the following account of the second escape attempt is from "Experiences of Air Service Officers": Hall, Mellen, Strong, Tucker, and Puryear; "Gefangenunterkunft auf der Burg Trausnitz, 1915–1918"; and Puryear, "Airman's Escape," pp. 460–64.

8. Puryear, "Airman's Escape," p. 463.

9. Ibid.

10. Ibid., p. 464.

11. Ibid.

12. Wolfgang W. Parth, *Vorwärts Kameraden, Wir müssen zurück*, p. 291.

13. Puryear, "Airman's Escape," pp. 461–62.

14. Ibid., p. 462.

VILLINGEN

1. Stadt Villingen-Schwenningen Stadtarchiv und Museen to the author 15 November 1991 and 17 January 1992; and the author's observations at the site, August, 1994.
2. George Puryear Papers; Gallagher Diary, 24 May 1918; Levere, *History of Sigma Alpha Epsilon*, pp. 332–33; and Isaacs, *Prisoner of the U-90*, pp. 87–89.
3. Ibid.
4. Isaacs, *Prisoner of the U-90*, p. 94; and "Camps, S-W Villingen."
5. Ibid.
6. After the Russians transferred out, Brown became the camp's senior officer ("Camps, S-W Villingen").
7. Ibid.
8. Isaacs, *Prisoner of the U-90*, pp. 94, 127.
9. George Puryear Papers; and Stadt Villingen-Schwenningen Stadtarchiv und Museen to the author, 15 November 1991 and 17 January 1992.
10. Dennett, *Prisoners of the Great War*, pp. 31–32; Robert Trudgett, "Hell Holes on Land and Sea," *Sunset*, May, 1919, p. 55; and Isaacs, *Prisoner of the U-90*.
11. Dennett, *Prisoners of the Great War*, p. 15.
12. Ibid., pp. 28–34; and Levere, *History of Sigma Alpha Epsilon*, p. 338.
13. Isaacs, *Prisoner of the U-90*, p. 122.
14. Ibid., pp. 122–23.
15. Ibid., p. 133; and George Puryear Papers.
16. Isaacs, *Prisoner of the U-90*, pp. 118–19.
17. Ibid., p. 124.
18. Ibid.
19. Trudgett, "Hell Holes on Land and Sea," pp. 54–55.
20. Ibid.
21. Isaacs, *Prisoner of the U-90*, pp. 101–103; and "Camps, S-W Villingen."
22. RG59, Microfilm Publication M367, roll 323, "Records of the Department of State Relating to World War I and its Termination," American Prisoners of War file (hereafter cited as M367 followed by the roll number and file name). Isaacs was so concerned that he might be falsely charged with escape while on parole that he kept his parole pass with him during his escape in October, 1918. If he were recaptured and so charged, he intended to use his parole pass to show that he had not given up his parole before escaping. His parole pass is among the Isaacs Family Papers.
23. Isaacs, *Prisoner of the U-90*, p. 129.
24. George Puryear Papers; and Puryear, "Airman's Escape," p. 615.

THE ESCAPE, 6 OCTOBER 1918

1. George Puryear Papers; Puryear, "Airman's Escape," p. 617; and Isaacs, *Prisoner of the U-90*.

2. Dennett, *Prisoners of the Great War*, p. 115; and "Camps, S-W Villingen."

3. Isaacs, *Prisoner of the U-90*, p. 150.

4. Ibid., p. 151.

5. George Puryear Papers.

6. Dennett, *Prisoners of the Great War*, p. 120; and Armstrong, ed., *Escape*, pp. 296–97.

7. George Puryear Papers.

8. "Experiences of Air Service Officers": Mellen, Rhodes, and Strong.

9. Ibid.

10. Dennett, *Prisoners of the Great War*, p. 124; and George Puryear Papers.

11. Gallagher Diary, 8 October 1918; Isaacs, *Prisoner of the U-90*; and Armstrong, ed., *Escape*, p. 297.

12. Gallagher Diary, 8 October 1918; Armstrong, ed., *Escape*, p. 297; and Dennett, *Prisoners of the Great War*, pp. 120–21.

13. George Puryear Papers.

14. Isaacs, *Prisoner of the U-90*, pp. 154–55.

15. Ibid., p. 155.

16. Ibid., p. 156.

17. Ibid.

18. George Puryear Papers; Puryear, "Airman's Escape," pp. 617–18; and "Experiences of Air Service Officers": Puryear.

19. "Experiences of Air Service Officers": Mellen and Strong.

20. Gallagher Diary, 8 October 1918.

21. Isaacs, "Special Report on Experiences."

22. George Puryear Papers.

23. Ibid.; and Puryear, "Airman's Escape," p. 618.

24. "Experiences of Air Service Officers": Mellen and Strong.

25. "Abschrift des Aussageprotokolls des amerikanischen Fliegeroberleutnants Rowan Tucker" 13 Oktober 1918 Buch XI/13/T. Bundesarchiv-Militärarchiv, Freiburg/Breisgau.

26. Puryear, "Airman's Escape," pp. 618–19.

27. "Experiences of Air Service Officers": Battle.

28. Puryear, "Airman's Escape," pp. 618.

29. Armstrong, ed., *Escape*, pp. 297–98; and Dennett, *Prisoners of the Great War*, pp. 122–23.

30. Dennett, *Prisoners of the Great War*, p. 124.

31. Armstrong, ed., *Escape*, p. 298; and Dennett, *Prisoners of the Great War*, p. 123.

32. "Experiences of Air Service Officers": Mellen and Strong.

33. Puryear, "Airman's Escape," pp. 618; and "Tatbericht Über die amerikanischen Offiziere 1) Isaacs, Edouard; 2) Battle, Blanchard [ergriffen]; 3) Puryear, George; 4) Tucker, Rowan [ergriffen]; 5) Willis Harold wegen gemeinschaftlicher Flucht und Suchbeschädigung," Nr.I/3605, 27 Oktober 1918.

34. Isaacs, *Prisoner of the U-90*, p. 159.

BATTLE

1. This account of Battle's evasion was taken entirely from "Tatbericht . . . Isaacs, Battle, Puryear, Tucker, and Willis"; and "Experiences of Air Service Officers": Battle.

TUCKER

1. This account of Tucker's evasion was taken entirely from "Abschrift . . . Tucker" and "Tatbericht . . . Isaacs, Battle, Puryear, Tucker, and Willis."

ISAACS AND WILLIS

1. Unless otherwise noted, the account of Isaacs's and Willis's evasion is found in Isaacs, *Prisoner of the U-90*, pp. 160–85; Armstrong, ed., *Escape*, pp. 289–316; and Dennett, *Prisoners of the Great War*, pp. 105–34.
2. Isaacs, *Prisoner of the U-90*, p. 162.
3. Armstrong, ed., *Escape*, p. 299.
4. As quoted in Dennett, *Prisoners of the Great War*, p. 124.
5. Ibid.
6. Isaacs, *Prisoner of the U-90*, p. 165.
7. Armstrong, ed., *Escape*, pp. 300–302.
8. Isaacs Testimony.
9. As quoted ibid., p. 125.
10. As quoted ibid., p. 126.
11. Ibid., p. 127.
12. Dennett, *Prisoners of the Great War*, p. 127.
13. Isaacs, *Prisoner of the U-90*, p. 170.
14. Ibid.
15. Ibid., p. 171.
16. As quoted in Armstrong, ed., *Escape*, p. 301.
17. Ibid.
18. Isaacs, *Prisoner of the U-90*, p. 172.
19. Ibid., p. 173.
20. Ibid., p. 174.
21. Ibid., p. 178.
22. As quoted in Armstrong, ed., *Escape*, p. 313.
23. As quoted in Armstrong, ed., *Escape*, p. 305.
24. Isaacs, *Prisoner of the U-90*, p. 181.

PURYEAR

1. Gallagher Diary, 8 October 1918.
2. "Tatbericht . . . Isaacs, Battle, Puryear, Tucker, and Willis."
3. Puryear, "Airman's Escape," pp. 619.
4. Ibid.
5. Ibid., p. 621.
6. Ibid.
7. Gallagher Diary, 8 October 1918.
8. Archibald, *Heaven High, Hell Deep*, pp. 307–308.
9. Puryear, "Airman's Escape," pp. 620.
10. Ibid.
11. Puryear Family Papers, no title, n.d., thirty-one-page typescript.
12. Puryear, "Airman's Escape," p. 621.
13. Ibid.
14. Ibid.
15. Ibid., p. 622.
16. Ibid.
17. George Puryear Papers.
18. Puryear, "Airman's Escape," p. 622.
19. Ibid.
20. George Puryear Papers.
21. Ibid.; and Puryear, "Airman's Escape," pp. 623–24.
22. Ibid.
23. Puryear, "Airman's Escape," p. 624.
24. Ibid.
25. Ibid.
26. Ibid.
27. Ibid.; and George Puryear Papers.
28. George Puryear Papers.
29. Puryear, "Airman's Escape," p. 625.
30. Ibid.
31. Dennett, *Prisoners of the Great War,* p. 134. The first American serviceman to reach Switzerland was Pvt. Frank Sovicki.
32. George Puryear Papers.
33. Ibid.

EPILOGUE

1. Puryear Family Papers.
2. "Experiences of Air Service Officers": Battle.
3. Ibid.

4. Michael J. Krisman, ed., *Register of Graduates and Former Cadets, 1802–1980*, p. 312.
5. Obituary, *San Diego Union*, 24 January 1990 and Isaacs Family Papers.
6. Gordon, *Lafayette Escadrille Pilot Biographies*, p. 175.
7. RG18, Records of the Army Air Force, 1907–1947, 9th Aero Squadron Operations, 11 August–3 November 1919, Military Reference Branch, NA.
8. "Puryear, George W., Report of Fatal Air Crash, 20 October 1919," Air Force Safety Agency, Norton Air Force Base, Calif.
9. Ibid.

Bibliography

PRIVATE PAPERS AND INTERVIEWS

Gallagher, Bernard James, M.D. Unpublished memoirs and diary in the possession of William B. Gallagher, M.D.

Gardner, Jennie. Interview and photographs by author, Nashville, Tenn., 1 December 1993.

Glasebrook, Col. C. R., U.S. Air Force (Ret.). Oral Histories, Papers and Artifacts of U.S. Army Air Service Pilots and Observers, 1917–18. The Glasebrook Foundation, Carson City, Nev.

Götze, Frank. Family papers. Berlin, Germany.

Gräbig, Lothar. Interview by author, Berlin, Germany, 16 August 1994.

Kranich, Kurt. Karlsruhe Stadthistoriker. Interview by author, Karlsruhe, Germany, 21 August 1994.

Parks, Allen. Family papers including George Puryear's photo albums, correspondence, and private papers, 1917–19.

Prangl, Josef. Staatliche Schlossverwaltung, Burg Trausnitz. Interview by author, 24 August 1994.

Puryear, William P. Interview by author, 23 February 1994, and family papers.

Reiss, Wolfgang. Stadtarchiv Rastatt, Interview by author, 22 August 1994, and correspondence, August–December, 1994.

Shackleford, Thaddeus. Private papers in the author's possession.

Thomson, Kenneth. Susie D. Franklin scrapbook.

Young, William Martin, Jr. Interview by author, Dixon Springs, Tenn., 18 March 1994.

U.S. GOVERNMENT DOCUMENTS

American Expeditionary Force.
"Tables of Organization, Air Service: Part I, Zone of Advance." 8 September 1918. Copy in author's possession.

An Act to Increase the Efficiency of the Aviation Service and for Other Purposes. U.S. House. 63d Cong., 2d sess., H.R. 5304, 18 July 1914.
Library of Congress, Washington, D.C.
    Mitchell, Gen. William. "From the Start to Finish of Our Greatest War." Reel no. 418685, General Mitchell's unedited wartime memoirs. "Mitchell Diaries"
National Archives, Washington, D. C.
    Civil Reference Branch
        RG59. Microfilm Publication M367, "Records of the Department of State Relating to World War I and its Termination, 1914–1929," American Prisoners of War file. Rolls 323, 324, and 325.
        RG76. Boundary and Claims Commissions Arbitration, Mixed Claims Commission United States and Germany.
            Case File 14689, Edouard Isaacs.
            Case File 11356, Herbert Allen Wardle.
        RG200. Records of the American National Red Cross, 1917–34. Files Pertaining to Bureau of Prisoners Information and Communication,
            6 April 1917 to 31 December 1918:
            Escaped American Prisoners
            Prisoners Notification and Classification Lists
            Prisoner Transfer Lists
            Death Reports
            Repatriation lists
        File 140.18, Bureau of Prisoners' Relief, 1917–1919, Part IV, "Camps, S-W Villingen."
    Military Reference Branch.
        RG18. Records of the Army Air Force, 1907–1947, boxes 612–36. 9th Aero Squadron Operations, 11 August–3 November 1919.
        RG45. Naval Records Collection, 1911–1927, Subject File USS *President Lincoln.*
        RG120. Microfilm Publication M990, "Gorrell's Histories of the American Expeditionary Forces Air Service, 1917–1919." Rolls 1, 16–21, 36, 41–42, and 44–46.
        RG242. Records of the German Navy, 1850–1945, Microfilm Publication T-1022, roll 614, PG61673, "Kriegstagebuch des Unterseebootes U-90."
National Personnel Records Center, St. Louis, Mo.
    "Statement of Service for Battle, Blanchard B."
    "Statement of Service for Puryear, George W."
    "Statement of Service for Tucker, Rowan H."
Norton Air Force Base, Calif. Air Force Safety Agency.
    "Puryear, George W. Report of Fatal Air Crash, 20 October 1919."
Special Regulations No. 43, "Officers' Reserve Corps Organized Under the National Defense Act of June 3, 1916," 16 June 1917. Copy in author's possession.

Special Regulations No. 50, "Aviation Section Signal Corps, 1917," 9 April 1917.
Copy in author's possession.
U.S. Army Military History Institute, Carlisle Barracks, Pa.
Thomas G. Miller Collection:
Gorman, Walter. *Book of Addresses of Officers and Enlisted Personnel of the 95th Aero Squadron, 1917–18.* n.d.
"History of the 95th Aero Squadron, 1918."
"96th Aero Squadron Daily Log, 12 June–7 December 1918."

COUNTY DOCUMENTS

Sumner County Archives, Gallatin, Tenn. "Puryear, George W., WWI Hero," History of Trousdale County.

GERMAN GOVERNMENT DOCUMENTS AND CORRESPONDENCE

Bayerischer Staatsarchiv, Burg Trausnitz, Landshut.
Schloss-Pflegerakten Landshut, Rep. 151, VIII Militär und Kriegsspital, File 101.
"Gefangenunterkunft auf der Burg Trausnitz, 1915–1918."
"Das K. Schloss Trausnitz: die Schliessung des Söllers," 26. March 1915. Nr. 6908.
"Bereitstellung von Räumen zur Unterbringung von Heeresgerät nach der Abrüstung," 3. Dezember 1915 Nr. 2775; 9. Dezember 1915 Nr. 1465; 10. Dezember 1915 Nr. 31; and 11. Dezember 1915 Nr. 1481.
Bayerische Verwaltung der staatlichen Schlösser, Gärten und Seen. "Landshut/Burg Trausnitz," 1993.
Bundesarchiv-Militärarchiv, Freiburg/Breisgau.
"Tatbericht Über die amerikanischen Offiziere 1) Isaacs, Edouard; 2) Battle, Blanchard [ergriffen]; 3) Puryear, George; 4) Tucker, Rowan [ergriffen]; 5) Willis Harold wegen gemeinschaftlicher Flucht und Suchbeschädigung," Nr.I/3605, 27 Oktober 1918.
"Abschrift des Zeugenaussageprotokolls Über den Fluchversuch des Amerikanischen Kapitänleutnants Isaacs," 19 Oktober 1929, Buch XIII/29.R.
"Abschrift des Zeugenaussageprotokolls Über den Fluchversuch des britischen Leutnants Charles Cook und des amerikanischen Leutnants Herbert Wardle," 5 August 1918," Buch IX/16.N.
"Abschrift des Aussageprotokolls des amerikanischen Fliegeroberleutnants Rowan Tucker" 13 Oktober 1918, Buch XI/13/T.
Generallandesarchiv Karlsruhe. Standort Karlsruhe.
"Offizier-Kriegsgefangenenlager und Lagerplan."
Stadt Karlsruhe, Stadtbibliothek, Archiv Sammlungen.

"Karlsruhe: Schicksalstage einer Stadt," von Kurt Kranich, 1973.
   Stadtplan Karlsruhe, 1920
Kreisstadt Rastatt. ·
   "Die Festung Rastatt."
Stadt Villingen-Schwenningen Stadtarchiv und Museen.
   Correspondence with the author, 15 November 1991–7 January 1992.

BOOKS

Air Force Historical Research Division, *U.S. Air Service Victory Credits in World War I.* USAF Historical Study no. 133. Maxwell Air Force Base, Ala.: USAF Historical Division, 1969.

American Battle Monuments Commission. *American Armies and Battlefields in Europe.* Washington, D.C.: GPO, 1938.

———. *American Battlefields in Europe.* Washington, D.C.: GPO, 1927.

Archibald, Norman. *Heaven High, Hell Deep: 1917–1918.* New York: A. and C. Boni, 1935.

Armstrong, H. C., ed. *Escape.* New York: Robert McBride, 1935.

Ayres, Leonard P. *The War With Germany: A Statistical Summary.* 2d ed. Washington, D.C.: GPO, 1919.

Bevan, Dr. W. L., and Dr. Hugo C. M. Wendel. *Harper's Pictorial Library of the World War.* 12 vols. New York and London: Harper and Brothers, 1920.

Bingham, Hiram. *An Explorer in the Air Service.* New Haven: Yale University Press, 1920.

Blodgett, Richard A. *The Life and Letters of Richard A. Blodgett, 1st Lieutenant United States Air Service.* Boston: MacDonald and Evans, 1919.

Buckley, Harold. *Squadron 95.* Paris: Obelisk, 1933

Chandler, Charles DeF., and Frank P. Lahm. *How Our Army Grew Wings.* New York: Roland, 1943.

Codman, Charles. *Contact: The History of the 96th Aero Squadron in the Great War.* Boston: Little, Brown, 1937.

Dennett, Carl P. *Prisoners of the Great War.* Boston and New York: Houghton Mifflin, 1919.

Ellenwood, Ralph E. *Behind the German Lines.* New York: Knickerbocker, 1921.

Ellis, John. *Eye Deep in Hell: Trench Warfare in World War I.* New York: Pantheon, 1976.

Fischdick, Arnold. *U-90: Kameradschaft und Erlebnisse im Ubootkrieg.* Essen: Walter Bachmeisters, 1937

Franks, Norman L. R., et al. *Above the Lines: A Complete Record of the Fighter Aces of the German Air Service, Naval Air Service and Flanders Marine Corps, 1914–1918.* London: Grub Street, 1993.

———. *The Jasta Pilots: Detailed Listings and Histories, August 1916–November 1918.* London: Grub Street, 1996.

Gerard, James W. *My Four Years in Germany.* New York: Grosset and Dunlop, 1917.

Glasebrook, Millie, ed. *American Aviators in the Great War, 1914–1918.* Carson City, Nev.: Glasebrook Foundation, 1984.

Goldberg, Alfred, ed. *A History of the United States Air Force, 1907–1957.* New York: London and Toronto: D. Van Nordstrand, 1957.

Gordon, Dennis. *Lafayette Escadrille Pilot Biographies.* Missoula, Mont.: Doughboy Historical Society, 1991.

Hallion, Richard P. *The Rise of the Fighter Aircraft, 1914–1918.* Baltimore: Nautical and Aviation, 1984.

Hennessy, Juliette A. *The United States Army Air Arm, April 1861–April 1917.* USAF Historical Studies No. 98. Maxwell Air Force Base, Ala.: USAF Historical Division, May, 1958.

Hudson, James J. *Hostile Skies: A Combat History of the American Air Service in World War I.* Syracuse, N.Y.: Syracuse University Press, 1968.

Isaacs, Edouard. *Prisoner of the U-90.* Boston and New York: Houghton Mifflin Co., 1919.

Jackson, Robert. *The Prisoners, 1914–18.* London: Routledge, 1989.

Jane's Fighting Aircraft of World War I. New York: Military Press, 1990.

Kennett, Lee. *The First Air War, 1914–1918.* New York: Free Press, 1991.

Kenney, George C., and Horace W. Guilbert. *History of the 91st Aero Squadron, U.S. Air Service.* Koblenz: Gebrüder Breamer, 1919.

Krisman, Michael J., ed. *Register of Graduates and Former Cadets, 1802–1980.* West Point, N.Y.: Association of Graduates, USMA, 1980.

Levere, William C. *The History of Sigma Alpha Epsilon in the World War.* Menasha, Wisc.: Collegiate, 1928.

Mauer, Mauer, ed. *The U. S. Air Service in World War I.* 4 vols. Washington, D.C.: GPO, 1978–79.

McCarthy, Daniel J. *The Prisoner of War in Germany.* New York: Moffat Yard, 1917.

McClung, Nellie. *Three Times and Out.* Boston and New York: Houghton Mifflin, 1918.

Mitchell, William. *Memoirs of World War I.* New York: Random House, 1960.

New England Aviators Publication Committee. *New England Aviators, 1914–1918.* Vol. 1. Boston and New York: Houghton Mifflin, 1919.

Newman, Basil. *Captured and Escaped.* Edinburgh and London: W. Blackwood and Sons, 1929.

Nowarra, Heinz J. *Eisernes Kreuz und Balken Kreuz.* Mainz: Dieter Hoffmann, 1968.

Parth, Wolfgang P. *Vorwärts Kameraden, Wir müssen zurück.* München: Deutscher, 1959.

Pyke, Geoffrey. *To Ruhleben and Back.* London: Constable, 1916.

Rickenbacker, Edward V. *Rickenbacker: An Autobiography.* Englewood Cliffs, N.J.: Prentice Hall, 1967.

Roosevelt, Kermit. *Quentin Roosevelt: A Sketch with Letters.* New York: Charles Scribner's Sons, 1921.

Russell, William M. *The Happy Warrior: Letters of William Muir Russell, an American Aviator in the Great War, 1917–1918.* Detroit: Saturday Night, 1919.

Sloan, James J., Jr. *Wings of Honor: A Compilation of all United States Pilots, Observers, Gunners and Mechanics Who Flew Against the Enemy in the War of 1914–1918.* Altglen, Pa.: Schiffer, 1994.

Speed, Richard B. *Prisoners, Diplomats, and the Great War: A Study in the Diplomacy of Captivity.* Westport, Conn.: Greenwood, 1990.

Sweeteser, Arthur. *The American Air Service.* New York and London: D. Appleton, 1919.

Thayer, Lt. Lucien H. *America's First Eagles: The Official History of the U.S. Air Service, A.E.F. (1917–1918).* Edited by Donald J. McGee and Roger J. Bender. San Jose, Calif., and Mesa, Ariz.: R. James Bender and Champlin Fighter Museum, 1983.

The Americans in the Great War: The Battle of St. Mihiel. Clermont-Ferrand: Michelin and Cie, 1920.

The Americans in the Great War: The Meuse-Argonne Battlefields. Clermont-Ferrand: Michelin and Cie, 1920.

The Americans in the Great War: The Second Battle of the Marne. Clermont-Ferrand: Michelin and Cie, 1920.

The Offensive of July 15, 1918. Fort Leavenworth, Kans.: General Service Schools Press, 1923.

Thomas, Ritchie, and Carl M. Becker, eds. *An American Pursuit Pilot in France: Roland W. Richardson's Diaries and Letters, 1917–1919.* Shippensburg, Pa.: White Mane, 1994.

Tucker, John. *Prisoner of War.* London: John Lane the Bodley Head, 1920.

Turner, John. *The Kaiser's Guest.* London: Edward Arnold, 1931. Beumelburg, Werner. *Sperrfeuer um Deutschland.* Oldenburg: Gerhard Stalling, 1929.

Tyler, H. W., ed. *Technology's War Record.* Cambridge: War Records Committee of the Alumni Association of MIT, 1920.

Woodward, David. *Armies of the World, 1854–1914.* New York: G. P. Putnam's Sons, 1978.

JOURNAL ARTICLES, NEWSPAPERS, AND MAGAZINES

Aero Age Weekly, 1917.

Commercial Appeal (Memphis, Tenn.), 13, 16, 17, 19, 21, 27, and 30 October 1918.

Eighmy, G. W., Jr. "Comments by Sumner Sewall, 95th U.S. Aero Squadron." *Cross and Cockade Journal* vol. IV, no. 4 (Winter, 1963): pp. 322–23.

Gill Robert B. ed. "The War Diaries and Letters of Walter W. Avery, and Lansing C. Holden Jr.—95th Aero Squadron." *Over the Front* vol. I, no. 3 (Fall, 1986): pp. 201–209.

Knowles, James. "Recollections." *Cross and Cockade Journal* X (Winter, 1969): pp. 355–65.

Puryear, George W. "The Airman's Escape." *Atlantic Monthly,* January and February, 1919, pp. 452–62, 615–27.

Trudgett, Robert D. "Hell Holes on Land and Sea." *Sunset,* May, 1919, pp. 30–32, 54–56, 99.

Index

clothing: civilian, 103, 104; disguise, 75, 113; uniforms, 6, 24, 28, 55, 59–60, 78, 129, 158

Coneau, André: escapes with Puryear, 58–61; French pilot, 58–59; uniform, 59; wants to steal German airplane, 60

Conflans, 36, 38

Cook, Capt. Charles F. (RAF): jumps from train, 24–25

Crowns, 2nd Lt. George H.: captured, 43; escape attempt, 55–58; escape failed, 124; at Karlsruhe main camp, 73; at Listening Hotel, 68; mentioned 61; recaptured, 58; tunnel, 98; uniform 55

Curry, 1st Lt. John "Rabbit" (pilot): ferry pilot, 22–23

disguises: civilian, 75; German soldier, 113; mentioned, 103, 141

doctors: American, 53, 58, 95, 119, 123; German, 81

Dubois, Pierre: plans Karlsruhe escape, 75

Duke, 2nd Lt. James (observer): captured, 37

Ehrt, Oberstleutnant: Villingen camp commandant, 155, 159

escape: conditions affecting, 56, 58, 101, 107; distraction during, 119–20, 123; fatigue, 117, 131, 146, 148, 150; groups, 55, 58, 83, 113–14; plans for, 83, 97; routes, 114, 116, 129, 134; rules for, 98, 165; uniform worn during, 24, 55, 59–60, 128

escape, useful items for: bed slats, 101–102; clothing, 99, 103, 116–17, 122, 128; compass, 58, 71, 77, 89, 118, 156, 157; digging tool, 83; food, 55, 56, 89, 99, 116, 128, 134–35; food found in the field, 117, 144, 146,

161; food from Red Cross parcels, 128, 134, 135, 160; hacksaw blade, 120; map, 55, 58, 71, 77, 81, 89, 100, 118, 128, 145, 156, 159; matches, 74, 156; money, 77; oil cloth, 74, 156; Pocket knife, 112, 156; rain gear, 55; Red Cross parcels, 99; wire, 102, 118; wire cutters, 102, 112, 118, 120

escapees, errors made by, 56, 58, 117–18, 130, 131, 136

escape attempts from: Eutin, 9; Friedrichsfeste, 55–58, 58–61; Karlsruhe Main Camp, 75–76, 77; mentioned, 13, 97; trains, 25–26, 79, 91; Trausnitz, 85–87, 87–89; Villingen, 97, 111–12

escape from: Eutin, 9–10; Friedrichsfeste, 55–59; Karlsruhe Main Camp, 74–77; Villingen, 97, 123–27

Eutin: described, 1–10; escape from, 9–10

Fokker. See aircraft

food: common topic among POWs, 64; found in the field, 117, 144, 146, 161; poor quality issued by Germans, 53, 66–67; supplied by Red Cross, 98–99, 102; used for escape, 55, 56, 89, 99, 116, 128, 134–35

Foote, Lt. Cdr. Percy W.: disguised as a coxswain, 12

Friedrichsfeste (Rastatt): area around, 54, 56; Chalmers and Crowns escape from, 55–58; described, 51–53; escapes easily made from, 53; escape procedure, 54–55; guards, 54–55, 59; Puryear and Coneau escapes from, 58–59

gas: poison, 40

guards: aboard trains, 24, 25, 78, 90; beat Isaacs, 79; beat Wardle, 26–27;

President Lincoln, USS: torpedoed, 12

Prisoners of War (POW): American, xi; treatment of by Germans, xii, 6, 7

Puryear, 1st Lt. George (pilot): captured, 46–47; encounter with civilians, 158, 163; escape attempts, 58–59, 87; escaped, 124–25; escape motive, 47, escape plans, 98; food, 160–61, 165; at Karlsruhe main camp, 71, 73; killed, 172; at Listening Hotel, 62, 68; quoted, 45, 59, 62, 71, 89, 92; rapid progress, 164; recaptured, 60–61; returned to AEF, 169; risks taken, xi, 156, 161, 162–63, 165; sick, 58, 90; solitary confinement, 107; swims across Rhine, 167–68; transferred to Villingen, 89; uniform 158

Raabe, Erich: German pilot, 34

Ratterman, 2nd Lt. George (observer): captured, 37

Red Cross: Camp Committee, 99; emergency parcels, 99; food parcels, 73, 98–99, 102; no supplies at Listening Hotel, 66: notification form, 62, 72

Remy, Kapitänleutnant Walter: searches for senior officer, 12–13; torpedoes *President Lincoln*, 12

Rhine: as escape goal, 57, 58, 116

Rhodes, 1st Lt. Carlyle "Dusty" (pilot): biography, 28; captured, 30; custom uniform, 28; escape attempts, 30; recaptured, 92; transfer, attempts to avoid, 90; transfer to Villingen, 89; tunnel, 98

Rickenbacker, Capt. Eddie (pilot), 33

Rosenfeld, Otto: German pilot, 34

Russians: American attitude toward, 97, 111; caused distraction, 119, 123; informants, 97, 100; moved out of Villingen, 111; orderlies, 97; at Villingen, 94–95, 100

Salmson. *See* aircraft

searches: area, 155; barracks, 77, 155; personal, 62, 71–72, 77, 79, 81; random, 51, 74

security: German internal, 58, 117

Schaffhausen salient: as escape goal, 116, 134, 159

Sovicki, Pvt. Frank, xii

Smith, 1st Lt. Herbert: lands at Burg, 37

solitary confinement: Friedrichsfeste, 61; Listening Hotel, 63, 66; Trausnitz, 87; Villingen, 79, 107

Strong, 2nd Lt. Alfred (observer): captured, 38; escape attempts, 39; escape failed, 124; escape plan, 113–15; transferred to Villingen, 89; at Trausnitz, 83; tunnel, 98

Thompson, 1st Lt. Syndey (pilot): killed, 29–30

Tichener, 2nd Lt. Caxton (observer): captured, 37; escape attempts, 39; escape failed, 126; escape plan, 113; transferred to Villingen, 89; tunnel, 98

Tracers: as interrogation technique, 19–20, 23

trains: description of, 23–24, 78, 90; guards aboard, 24, 25, 78, 90; jumps from, 25–26, 79, 91; POW behavior aboard, 24; used for POW transport, 23–24, 78, 90; use of rejected at Villingen, 115–16

Trausnitz Castle: description, 80–81, 83; escape attempts from, 85–86, 87–89; inoculations at, 81–82; Mr. Capp, 81–82, 83; POW quarters in, 82; searches in, 81; window bars easily removed, 84

Trudget, Capt. Robert D.: Merchant Marine officer, 104

Tucker, 2nd Lt. Rowan (observer): captured, 37; court-martialed, 170–71;

escape attempt, 110; escaped, 124; escape plans, 98, 111; slow progress, 135, 136, 137; recaptured, 139; rendezvous with battle, 128; at Trausnitz, 83
tunnel 98, 101

U-90, 11, 12
uniforms: Battle, 129; Chalmers and Crowns, 55; Isaacs's similar to French, 73; officer's uniform supplied to Willis, 6; Puryear, 59; Rhodes's custom, 28; worn during escapes, 24, 55, 59–60, 129

Villingen: becomes an American camp, 95; description, 93–95, 96–97; escape attempts from, 97, 111–12; guards, 94, 95, 98, 100, 105, 112, 121, 125; orderlies in, 97; parole passes issued, 104–105; parole walks allowed, 103, 105–106; Russians in, 94–95, 100; security in, 93, 95, 97

Wardle, 1st Lt. Herbert (pilot): beaten by guards, 27; biography, 21–22; captured, 23; escape attempt, 26; escape failed, 125; escape plan, 113; ferry flight, 21–23; recaptured, 26–27
Waldshut: as escape goal, 53, 116, 141, 158
Williamson, Capt. Joseph (observer): captured, 18; at Karlsruhe main camp, 72
Willis, Sgt. Harold (pilot): biography, 5; captured, 5–6; delirious, 149–50; encounters with civilians, 145, 147, 149, 150, 151; escape attempts, 9–10; escaped, 125; escape plan, 98, 113; Lafayette Escadrille pilot, 5; meets with Isaacs, 141; returns home, 169, 171; swims across Rhine, 153–54; WWII service, 171